Journey to the Edge of the Woods

Journey to the Edge of the Woods

Women of Cultures Healing From Trauma

Christine Graef
Foreword by Willie Jock

WIPF & STOCK · Eugene, Oregon

JOURNEY TO THE EDGE OF THE WOODS
Women of Cultures Healing From Trauma

Copyright © 2015 Christine Graef. All rights reserved. Except for brief quotations in critical publications or reviews, no part of this book may be reproduced in any manner without prior written permission from the publisher. Write: Permissions, Wipf and Stock Publishers, 199 W. 8th Ave., Suite 3, Eugene, OR 97401.

Wipf & Stock
An Imprint of Wipf and Stock Publishers
199 W. 8th Ave., Suite 3
Eugene, OR 97401

www.wipfandstock.com

ISBN 13: 978-1-4982-0858-1

Manufactured in the U.S.A.

Scripture quotations marked (NIV) are taken from the Holy Bible, New International Version®, NIV®. Copyright © 1973, 1978, 1984, 2011 by Biblica, Inc.™ Used by permission of Zondervan. All rights reserved worldwide. www.zondervan.com The "NIV" and "New International Version" are trademarks registered in the United States Patent and Trademark Office by Biblica, Inc.

"Those who look to him are radiant; their faces are never covered with shame" (Ps 34:5).

Contents

Foreword by Willie Jock: A Vision Unfurled | ix
Introduction | xi

1 *Shadows* | 1
2 *The Woods Edge* | 21
3 *Through Fields of Harvest* | 42
4 *Community* | 59
5 *The Covenant of Forgiveness* | 77
6 *The Longhouse* | 95
7 *Mothers of Nations* | 115

Bibliography | 131

Foreword
A Vision Unfurled

December 11, 2012—7:30 am: While praying this morning with my wife I received a vision from the Lord. In the vision I heard the voice of God say to me, "Look at this my son." Then I saw huge hands unfurl the most beautiful tapestry I've ever seen. Words fail me to describe the beauty of this tapestry. I marveled at the colors of blue, purple, and scarlet. There was also silver and gold thread throughout. It was absolutely breathtaking.

"Why is it not hanging in a prominent place in heaven?" I asked. Then I heard, "In its design it is completed, but it is incomplete." But to me it looked completed so I asked, "Isn't it completed?"

"No, look closely and you will notice the many gaps and holes in it." I had to really look hard for any imperfections, and then I saw them. The more I looked the more I saw.

"What caused all the holes?" I asked.

"Un-forgiveness," I was told. Whenever there is a major release of forgiveness here on earth a hole is woven closed. As I watched I could actually see weaving taking place. As I looked closer at the fabric, each thread was made up of people. The whole tapestry was alive with movement. I could see forgiveness taking place right before me.

I believe that the First Nations people have a huge role in seeing this tapestry finished. As we see the power of forgiveness released, we see healing released in the same measure.

—Willie Jock, Bear Clan Mohawk, Akwesasne

Introduction

Women's rights activist Matilda Joslyn Gage was given the name *Karonienhawi* ("Sky Carrier") by the Mohawk Wolf Clan after she was arrested in 1893 for trying to vote in a school board election. Gage lived in upstate New York with her contemporaries, Elizabeth Cady Stanton and Lucretia Mott, where they forged friendships with the original people of the land, the six nations of the Haudenosaunee Confederacy. From east to west they are the Mohawk, Oneida, Onondaga, Cayuga, Seneca, and later the Tuscarora.

These early American women came from a culture of Comstock Laws forbidding discussion of marital rape. Under church and state, women had no custody of their own children and no ownership of land or money. They could not sign contracts or have a voice in voting. Seeing that the women were treated in ways against their own tradition, the native people came to think of the church as another institution against them.

Living side by side with the native women, the Euro-American women witnessed how responsibilities were shared among the men and women of the village. It was clan mothers who nominated the *roiane* ("chiefs")—a man who the community agrees is of good character and known to put the needs of others before his own. He cannot have committed theft, murder, or assault on a woman. Husbands and wives provided for each other, he cared for her family and she gave time to help in the fields of his family.

Introduction

Stanton had frequent dinners with the Oneida women. Gage watched nearby Onondaga women planting and harvesting nutritious foods for their families. Mott and her husband James worked on a committee of Quakers who helped prevent territory of the Seneca from being illegally taken from them. They all saw how women shared in discussions about decisions in their nations. They experienced men holding the women in great respect in a matrilineal society that passes lineage through the women because they, like Earth, are the life-givers.

In the 1970s when Dr. Sally Roesch Wagner researched these women she wondered what had inspired them to transform the world with their suffragette movement. Divorce laws began to change by the end of the nineteenth century. The Married Women's Property Acts gradually were enacted. Women got the right to vote, the right to choose careers and keep their children.

Wagner, one of the first American women to earn a doctorate in women's studies, found their inspiration came from what they absorbed by knowing the native women. As the country's foremost authority on Matilda Joslyn Gage, Sally Wagner is Executive Director of the Gage Foundation in upstate New York and teaches this history often on stages with Jeanne Shenandoah, daughter of Onondaga Deer Clan Mother Audrey and a midwife.

Wagner researched Mott's travels to Seneca Falls where she and Stanton held the world's first women's rights convention. Mott wrote several articles for the *New York Evening Post* about the Haudenosaunee ways of equal responsibilities between the sexes. Stanton was called a heretic, an enemy of the church for advocating the natural childbirth practices of the Haudenosaunee and divorce laws that would free women from abusive marriages. In those days, police would return a woman fleeing a violent husband. They were considered to be possessions with the status of a slave. In 1893, Gage wrote in *Woman, Church, and State*, "In the name of religion the worst crimes against humanity have ever been perpetrated."[1] Beginning a different perspective of the bible, Stanton agreed, writing, "Christianity putting the religious weapon

---

1. Gage, *Woman, Church, State*, 263.

Introduction

into man's hand made his conquest complete."² Indian women were much better off than women under white man's law.

Haudenosaunee women today continue to nominate the leaders who represent them. They still have the power to remove him if he does not abide by the best for his people. Because they have worked with the men throughout the past onslaught of wars, assimilation policies, and environmental poisoning, their nation's teachings continue to be passed to the next generations.

Their struggle today is with historic traumas that press down on their families with addiction, abuse, suicides, children taken from their families, and violence. As their grandmothers and mothers did before them, the women gather to talk about the wellness of their people. They come together by the rivers, in the longhouses, around kitchen tables, during conferences and in rehab centers. They remember the unique image of God created to be male and female balances.

Discussions turned to strategies of hope as they found ways in their heritage to nurture well being together. This became a thread of healing in the tapestry women weave with other cultures. As they each looked back through the years to what their ancestors had carried forward for them, they found a collective power in their origins.

2. Stanton, "Antagonisms of the Sexes," 259.

1

Shadows

On the evening of March 26, I drove to the local police department where I live in New York. Inside I was arrested, finger printed, and mug shots were taken. I'm full of shame. I feel like a criminal. But I don't regret it. My charge was harassment. For months I had phoned and emailed a man I learned had sexually abused children in his community and I'd been warning others about him. I'd unknowingly gotten involved with a child molester whom I'll call "B." He was on probation for attempting to molest a ten-year-old girl and I hadn't known.

—Millie, after discovering a man she worked with was a pedophile. He took her to court to silence her from speaking about the women whom he had abused.

After the breach of God's guidance came into the world, Adam and Eve's relationship with God was forever changed. They had lost the closeness with him they'd enjoyed. But they had not forgotten him. When Eve bore her first son, Cain, full of awe she said, "With the help of the Lord I have brought forth a man" (Gen 4:1).

Eve cried the first teardrops of a grieving woman when Cain murdered his brother Abel in a jealous rage and had to leave, becoming a wanderer far from his mother and father. Realizing that God can restore the broken life came when she birthed another son, Seth, Eve said, "God has granted me another child in place of Abel, since Cain killed him" (Gen 4:25). Adam and Eve would live brokenhearted knowing that by ignoring God's instruction, they had caused the loss of their sons, both Cain and Abel, but they had continued speaking to their children of the Lord who had given them life. When Seth was born, "At that time people began to call on the name of the Lord" (Gen 4:26), Adam and Eve told them of God's promise to send someone to restore the balance.

> And I will put enmity between you and the woman, and between your offspring and hers; he will crush your head, and you will strike his heel (Gen 3:15).

In Adam and Eve, God created a unique image of himself when he created male and female, a union that brings about God's design. To break apart the plan, the enemy's first attack in the new creation was to target the woman Eve. Tempting her to eat of the tree of knowledge that God told Adam and Eve was not good to eat, the enemy of God lied. The lie was "you are not enough."

The lie has targeted women in every generation in every community worldwide to erase God's plan for her. In South Dakota in 2014 a Lakota elder told of finding "a crying, naked, four-year-old girl running" down one of the roads outside of the Man Camp of workers along an oil pipeline. The little girl had been sexually assaulted. In Winnipeg, Canada a fifteen-year-old aboriginal girl was found dead wrapped in a bag and dumped in the Red River. In 2008, two indigenous girls in the Philippians, aged thirteen and fourteen, were gang raped by soldiers while on their way to school. Three years later, reports surfaced of twelve boys and eight girls, aged four to seventeen, being abducted for ransom to finance armed groups. Cries from the stories of recurrent gang rape, enslavement, and killing of tribal women rise from Myanmar in Southeast Asia. Guatemala, a country of social transition after decades of armed conflict, reported the bodies of 705 women found mutilated, violated, and dumped in public places as a message of warning to communities. All around the world the cries of death, violence, and exploitation are coming from women of every race and culture.

The curse of lies brought about by a fallen world that was separated from God. So God raised up Jeremiah to speak to the people. Anguished over the city of Zion, the daughter of his people, suffering from immorality in their minds and their relationships, Jeremiah wept.

> Since my people are crushed, I am crushed;
> I mourn, and horror grips me. Is there no balm in Gilead?
> Is there no physician there?
> Why then is there no healing for the wound of my people? (Jer 8:21–22).

The daughter of God's people today suffer desperate wounds from the complications of a fallen world described in Isa 1:6 as having "only wounds and welts and open sores, not cleansed or bandaged or soothed." Knowledge of the physician, Jesus, has been on the North American continent for centuries. Then why, as Jeremiah asked, isn't the daughter of the people healed? "The harvest is past, the summer is ended, and we are not saved!" (Jer 8:20).

As Christians approach Indian reservations wanting to bring the balm, they meet a people whose experience of church had been as a force come to stifle their giving thanks, silence their songs of worship, or break up their families. These are territories where intense efforts are recovering traditional knowledge and language guarding against white man's method of living. In Millie's land, as on other reserves, there are elders who know the Christ, and neighbors who believe the Son of God. But they won't call themselves Christians. "Christian" is a word associated with no longer being an Indian; it is a word associated with past church behavior.

Millie's encounter with a child abuser brought memories from her own unguarded hours of childhood, tearing at her heart. She began, at fifty years old, to seek a way to heal. Unspoken, a psalm yearned in her heart with prayer Eve would have understood.

> You are my hiding place;
> you will protect me from trouble
> and surround me with songs of deliverance (Ps 32:7).

Millie wouldn't seek the help of a Bible or a church. A Mohawk woman from Akwesasne in northeastern New York, she knows the devastation that the early religion committed on the first people of the land. When Europeans arrived on the continent, the Haudenosaunee wove the Two-Row Wampum, a belt of white beads with two purple rows running parallel through is length, symbolizing the two cultures with the language, laws, and customs in the European ship and those of the people of the canoe. Three white rows separating the two vessels represent the friendship, peace, and respect that are to guide each as we travel the rivers of life side by side.

As the years went by, however, the three rows began to disappear. The concept of respect that bound the two vessels to each other faded as the population of the new countries of America and Canada expanded. In Europe the monarchs were using religion to establish a centralized power of unity, causing divisions and persecutions by both Protestants and Catholics. Dissenters we tortured, beaten or burned to death, strangled, and imprisoned if they disagreed with established doctrine.

Others were banished. By the 1890s more than half of the immigrants in the United States were Europeans from religiously oppressed countries. The thought that one culture is necessary to unity grew with the new societies and government began policies of assimilating Indians, taking away their children to place in boarding schools or adopted out to non-native families.

Laws were established against their own language, prayers, and customs. The people were mocked, scoffed at, and persecuted. This is remembered among the first people of the land. These are footprints through history, shadows that all but stamped out indigenous people discovering the life of Christ whose ways were not the conquests of others, but a protocol based on respect, friendship, and peace.

> Therefore I exhort, first of all, that supplications, prayers, intercessions, *and* giving of thanks be made for all men, for kings and all who are in authority, that we may lead a quiet and peaceable life in all godliness and reverence. For this *is* good and acceptable in the sight of God our Savior (1 Tim 2:1–3).

As a member of the Kanien'kehá:ka (People of the Place of Flint)—often called the Mohawk Nation that has communities in northeastern New York and southern Ontario—Millie descends from a people who say that what makes our Creator cry also makes a woman cry. Alcohol, drug use, and mind changers that disconnect a person from clear thinking; harming a child; witchcraft bringing mean-spirited intent against someone; lies that break a person's heart, causing the mind to harden.

The Mohawk are the eastern gatekeepers of the six nations Haudenosaunee, also known as the Iroquois, a league that joined the Mohawk, Oneida, Onondaga, Cayuga, Seneca, and Tuscarora into a confederacy centuries ago.

Out of these generations of wounds to their communities, women are re-weaving the threads that bind the Two-Row Wampum, the respect and friendship of recognizing two different cultures through sharing stories of the struggles of children and the role of women in the creation. In the fall of 2013, Akwesasne hosted more than 250 child welfare professionals representing some fifty community, tribal, county, state and federal agencies, and drawing representatives from the Department of Homeland Security, US Border and Customs Protection, US Marshall Service and the US Attorney's Office. The forum, the first annual Child Safe Summit, was a collaboration with Dr. Karyn Patno, a pediatrician and founder of the Child Safe Program at Fletcher Allen Health Care in Burlington, Vermont.

Presentations shared disturbing forensic photographs, x-rays of injuries, digital child exploitation, cyber-bullying, and brought discussion of the continuing need for people to open their eyes and see it happening around them.

They spoke of how the moment passes like a shooting star when someone chose not to help a child. A life lived knowing no one heard her cry ripples through the community, revealed in emails to Millie as she began finding more girls who had been victimized:

> "Yes I know of two girls that never said anything. I don't bother with him at all."
>
> "I even quit going to longhouse because I don't want to see them there."
>
> "They too often say, 'It's not my business, I don't want to get in the middle of this.' But if we all stood together like in old days we'd be saying this is unacceptable. Now we feel on our own."
>
> "There's some counseling available but if I go everyone knows and whispers about it."
>
> "Our communities are tight-knit. A lot of people don't want to go against each other."
>
> "They became afraid to speak out if it's about someone they know or it risks their job."
>
> "I hear the problem isn't dealt with because it would hurt our programs."

Gravity is heavier here. Prayer asks for protections to survive until prophecies are fulfilled. Knowing that the worst can happen and enemies do not go away, prayer is for each generation to take up the struggle. Hardship of every kind assaults the community. A hundred million deaths occurred in the Americas between 1492 and 1890. The people of the continent lost millions of acres fraudulently to the newcomers. Pollution of their waters and lands by neighboring industries forced a sustainable life to become one of store bought foods causing rates of diabetes and heart disease to be higher than national averages. Racism and fear prevented men from being hired locally and many men left their families to work in construction in other states, visiting home only when they could. Drugs have infiltrated their youth. Organized crime has found participants to smuggle weapons, drugs, alcohol, cigarettes, and humans across the border.

There are more than seventy thousand Mohawk living on seven territories: Ganienkeh, Kanesatake, Kahnawake, Tyendinaga, Wahta, Ohsweken, and Akwesasne. The generation today is troubled with accelerating assaults and murders of females. In Indian country the rate is an alarming 2.5 times higher than the national average, manifested in rising substance abuse, suicides, and depression's unseen tears. Sexual and emotional abuse of children has become commonplace.

Women sat together in kitchens, gathered at conferences, shared stories as they took walks together, recalling the strength of their grandmothers, remembering elders who as couples were leaders in the community, still holding hands, laughing together, talking of a vibrant community supporting families that assured the sovereignty of their future as a people. The scent of sweetgrass growing on the riverbanks, still picked to weave with ash splints into traditional baskets, reminded of earth and their mothers' hands. They remembered land links with health, flowing in a continuous cycle supporting the body's well being and the mind's creativity. They spoke about how health and legal systems provide treatment only as needed for each ailment.

They talked of the need for well being to encompass an individual from family to community, to the natural world, and the spiritual. The region is under a stronghold. Special Agent Tim Losito of the Homeland Security Department told the attendees gathered in Akwesasne that the Northern District of New York prosecutes more child exploitation cases than anywhere else in the United States. Tribal Chief Beverly Cook said this emphasizes the importance of communication and collaboration between all communities.

Members of social services, law enforcement, medical, mental health, alcohol and chemical dependency, domestic violence formed the Onkwahwatsire (Our Family) Multidisciplinary Team and supported the Child Safe Summit.

Journey to the Edge of the Woods

"Collaboration is second nature to most women and service organizations," Karonienhawi "Hawi" Thomas said.[1] Hawi is an investigator for the tribal police and member of the Konon:kwe Council, a women's circle for social change "from the seeds and at the roots" of extended families in Akwesasne. Rooted in the Haudenosaunee's matrilineal kinship system, the Konon:kwe Council encircles girls and women with cultural knowledge that strengthens the dignity of women critical to family and community. The Council is a lead agency in the Child Safe summits. Its mission states, "Our foundational commitment is to Mohawk sovereignty, self-determination and community resilience. This is the basic context for the safety of Mohawks, beyond the systemic barriers of discrete programs and agencies."

Creative partnerships extended to the National Center on Domestic Violence, Trauma and Mental Health, New York State Coalition Against Sexual Assault, Native Youth Sexual Health Network, Indigenous Youth and Elders Circle, and the National Museum of the American Indian. The Women's Circle also presents leadership in the Smithsonian Institution's Patterns of Native Health and Wellbeing Symposium. Traditions are shared among when partners of the National Indigenous Women's Resource Center to develop curriculum for community-based domestic violence advocates.

They are committed to upholding the inherent identity of women.

Millie's perception of being a beautiful creation of God had distorted when the bonds of trust were betrayed. She reached for the teachings of the *onkwehonwe* (people who have original knowledge) grandmothers who had left a light burning so they could find their way home. Centuries ago Millie's people were brought out of vicious battles, revenge killings, and violence that left women terrified to walk outside their doors. An answer came, a thousand years after Christ walked the earth, when a man known as Skennenrahawi (He Carries the Peace) came to the battle-fatigued people.

1. "Beyond the Shelter Doors."

Shadows

The Peacemaker was a Huron-born on the north shores of Lake Ontario. Led by a vision he crossed the lake in his canoe into what later became New York State. He went first to the Mohawk people where they lived in villages along the Mohawk River Valley and east into the Adirondack Mountains. The Mohawk were the first to recognize their own actions and forgive the wrongs that had happened and they accepted the Kaianerekowa, the new governance of the Great Law of Peace. Peacemaker followed the river currents to the Oneida, Onondaga, Cayuga and Seneca to bring all five nations into a League that would survive the onslaught of centuries of genocide, assimilation policies, environmental toxins, and religious attempts to convert them. The Tuscarora who live by the Niagara River joined the Confederacy in the 1700s.

When he came, Peacemaker met Aiionwatha (Hiawatha) whose grief from the murders of his three daughters had isolated him. Aiionwatha sat by himself at a lake stringing shells and speaking words of comfort with each string he lay across a pole, saying if he ever met anyone who was as broken-hearted as he felt, he would speak these words to them. Hearing him, Peacemaker went to him, picked up the strings of wampum and spoke to Aiionwatha the words he'd heard him say. His understanding transformed Aiionwatha's heart.

Peacemaker used this to bring a way to understand the process of pain and the path out of its shadows. His belief for Aiionwatha's well-being reaffirmed that there is purpose for his life, a strategy that Aiionwatha became responsible for as he in turn would bring the empathy to others in a world that had killed his daughters and unborn grandchild. This compassion became observed in the Edge of the Woods Ceremony that shares the weariness of grieving. It begins as a group set off through the forest to meet with others. They walk along a path of pine needles and leaves, singing a melody as if each fallen leaf is the name of an ancestor who made the journey possible for them today.

Millie looked down this path of her ancestors and determined to follow the footsteps they left to reach the place of sunlight. As she stepped deeper into the path, heavy shadows of loneliness fell across her mind. On the way to the edge of the woods she would pass under many shadows, much the way the seven nations of Israel had to subdue the giants to reach the Promised Land (Josh 3:10). Just as in the Hebrew story of Joshua's perseverance passed down to us, protocols help us understand there are influences of other cultures that could prevent our journey: Canaanites we will encounter, a name that means merchants, that can distract our sight to look for satisfaction in consumerism. There were Hittites bringing discouragement by clouding the words of truth. Hivites are like imposter plants appearing to have medicine but offer alternative beliefs to lure people away from God's instructions. The people had to discern the Perizzites, a people who had separated from their place in community with words spoken apart from the whole. Then there were the Girgashites, people who kept returning to living without spiritual guidance. The Israelites had to discipline thought and word to pass through the Amorites and not become like their arrogance and boasting or Jebusites who defiled others with oppressions.

It is the path walked by the poor in spirit; those who mourn; the humble; those who hunger and thirst for righteousness; the merciful; the pure in heart; the peacemakers; and the persecuted (Matt 5:5–11).

The poor and needy search for water, but there is none; their tongues are parched with thirst. But I the Lord will answer them; I, the God of Israel, will not forsake them (Isa 41:17).

Since the time Adam and Eve were separated from the Lord, God has spoken continually to the exiled and those who are far from him. He sends prophets to deliver the message of a future. He speaks his promise through nature when the light of sun softens the frozen landscape and brings new growth. He brings teachers to prepare our understanding.

With joy you will draw water from the wells of salvation (Isa 12:3).

As Millie's steps went forward she saw sunlight slanting on the forest floor where an abundance of flowers, seeds, and plants in the underbrush were there to strengthen her. Where she saw

Shadows

poison ivy she found jewelweed growing nearby to ease the discomfort of itch. Balsam Fir offered antiseptic pitch to cover abrasions. The inner bark of the Tamarack could be boiled with leaves for tea for sore throats. Winterberry's dark green leaves growing close to the ground offer treatment for fever and white blooms become edible red berries. Millie saw that even in shadows God had placed plants growing together in shaded communities with bracken ferns that could repel insects and White Trillium, whose frame of green leaves can be cooked for nourishment.

In times of old her elders walked along singing a melody that mourned for the grandmothers and grandfathers who had upheld their constitution. They knew that if they didn't preserve these ways it could be lost to the people and times of battling and fear could return.

Concern for the misery of the abused would bring mercy to Millie's own tears. But as she began, she thought that God was silent. He had not been there for her when she had been a child abused by those older. He was not answering her cry for justice against the man she knew harmed little girls.

Far above us, above the stars, he "who dwells in unapproachable light" (1 Tim 6:16) understood this. Jesus deliberately waited as Millie's prayers became less about getting answers and turned toward wanting to know God's presence.

This is my comfort in my affliction, that your promise gives me life (Ps 119:50).

They arrive from the journey through the woods to be met by a delegation who perform the ceremony lifting the burden of trauma so the beauty around them again can help them continue on and make good decisions. In turn the weary travelers who arrived perform the ceremony for those who had addressed them.

The reciprocal protocol brings both to be concerned with each other and gave women a voice for all time to come. The league has nine clans dispersed in each nation—turtle, wolf, deer, bear, eel, hawk, beaver, heron, and snipe. A child is born into the clan of the mother, progenitors of life. Each clan has a *kontiianehson* (clan mother) who holds a string of wampum authorizing her to nominate a *roiane* (he upholds the peace) for her clan, also called a chief. As women out among the community watching children grow they recognize who is trustworthy, honest, takes care of his family, and knows his heritage.

When the men and women both agree on a candidate for their clan they submit his name to the other clans for confirmation and then to the *roianes* (chiefs) of each clan. Then it's brought to the *roiane* of the other five nations. When it's agreed, the title is conferred with a ceremony that brings Aiionwatha's condolence into practice for the leadership.

O-ne-kor-ha, a set of wampum strings, symbolizes the equal contributions of the women and men vesting the title, a position that carries responsibility toward the land and people so that each generation will continue in peace.

This constitution would sustain them as darkness filled their future.

In the community, men and women acted in one accord in male and female roles. This was not the idea of the church. This was God's design for every culture around earth.

So God created man in his own image, in the image of God he created him; male and female he created them (Gen 1:27).

No amount of political correctness or policy changes by church or government can move God to change just to accommodate us.

Drink water from your own cistern, running water from your own well (Prov 5:15).

Each generation must renew and uphold it.

And Isaac dug again the wells of water that they had dug in the days of Abraham his father, for the Philistines had stopped them up after the death (Gen 26:18).

A well cannot be filled from the outside. It must be dug deeply, internally, personally, to find the living streams that are the words and Spirit of God. On the last day of the Festival of Tabernacles, Jesus, usually a soft-spoken man, stood up amid the crowd of singing and dancing people and said in a loud voice, "Let anyone who is thirsty come to me and drink. Whoever believes in me, as Scripture has said, rivers of living water will flow from within them" (John 7:37–38). He was giving them a promise to take with them when the day of rejoicing was over, words to carry home to their daily lives and the sorrows, losses, or betrayals that come. He was giving a message to remember when they came to the moments of thirsting.

Through the living waters God calls on women to mourn together, to rejoice, to teach, to sing, and dance. He said, "our daughters will be like pillars carved to adorn a palace" (Jer 144:12). Because the dust of the world coats our sight, our hearing, and our voices every day, traditions are kept to transform our minds back to thoughts of serving God. We are called, not to assimilate another person into our way of living, but to prepare the way, an example set by John the Baptist as we come with our despair and hope to the water baptism. John turned people to focus heavenward to touch the hem of the priest chosen by God who is able to make a way for our brokenness.

But when the new country founded itself on the North American continent, the native people of the land saw the way Comstock Laws permitted men to abuse and oppress women using religion to justify it. Their high esteem of women as life givers wanted no part of that kind of god. The Haudenosaunee constitution provides a need for both a female and a male faithkeeper for each clan who sit in council with the clan mothers and *roiane*. Together they share the responsibilities of the times to gather in the longhouse and bring thanks. Clan mothers need to be present for a ceremony to begin. They supervise the procedures and the foods needed. The act of naming a newborn baby is given to the clan mother at these times, binding her as a power of influence in the child's life.

The Mohawk Nation of Akwesasne, where Millie lives, encompasses New York State, Quebec, and Ontario with a population of about fourteen thousand people. It was named Akwesasne (land where the ruffed grouse drums) centuries ago when nature abounded and the fresh water of the St. Lawrence River was clear and healthy flowing from the Great Lakes through their community. Forests provided fire, shelter, and a bounty of fruits and nuts.

Journey to the Edge of the Woods

Meadows drenched with morning dew from the warmth of earth meeting the coolness of the sky gave wild asparagus, onions, wild peas, garlic, and a variety of medicinal plants.

The border between Canada and the United States was drawn through the St. Lawrence River with the 1794 Jay Treaty. New York State used guns and imprisonment early in the 1800s to force the men to establish the elected system of the St. Regis Mohawk Tribe. Despite repeated objections to the point of death, Canada enforced the Mohawk Council of Chiefs. The traditional Longhouse Council as Peacemaker established continues under the season's cycles.

The government and church acknowledgment of past wrongs has not affected much change between the native and non-native governments. On the one-year anniversary of Canada's official apology to First Nations for the residential school system, a gathering of government officials and the Assembly of First Nations convened on Parliament Hill in 2009 to commemorate National Reconciliation Day. Questioning what exactly has been reconciled, Tim Thompson, Grand Chief of the Mohawk Council of Akwesasne, stood and called Canada's Public Safety Minister Peter Van Loan "a liar" for claiming to have carried out consultations with the community of Akwesasne about the plan to arm border agents with guns on their territory. Someone commented, "It's inevitable that someone's going to get shot."[2]

Surrounded on every side by another people's ways of living, they were seeing youth become dismissive of their elders. The joy in little girls giggling at the wonder of life around them quieted in schools by friends who have more material goods or better grades, unkind groups, or becoming victims of disturbed grown-ups. Some turned into women who lure men into wounding their family relationships, others unprotected by mother or father becoming lonely no matter who is at their side.

Women in Akwesasne looked back to the days Peacemaker was among them, calming a great anger and retrieving each person from their isolation. They spoke of renewals with knowledge gained from the environment around them showing the promise

---

2. Cuffe, "A Declaration of War."

Shadows

of God's intent. Trust in the sky over them and the earth beneath their feet revealed that the foundations of higher natural law had not changed. Creator dwells in the relationship between mankind and nature manifested in the evening star or when a baby is born. This Great Mystery covers the children wherever they go, the eagles wherever they fly, the fish however deep they swim. Fish were dying because of toxins from industries destroying their river culture. Children were unhealthy and under constant threat of physical and sexual abuse from the world around them. Elders, once pioneers who brought nurturing, were becoming survivors lamenting the behaviors of the youth. But God's design for well being had not changed.

Millie attended a community presentation given by Hawi who spoke about recognizing the stages predators move through using words to groom their prey until they overcome their guards. Spotting a vulnerable woman in a troubled marriage, lonely for so long, B targeted Millie with flattering words she ached to hear. She liked who she was when she was with him. But she had chosen an imposter plant, poisonous, and not the true medicinal plant.

They are clouds without rain, blown along by the wind, autumn trees, without fruit and uprooted—twice dead (Jude 1:12).

> *When the local law enforcer did her presentation on the issue I could identify with all the feelings of children and women who've been violated. What this man does is with the intent to hurt women and young girls. He said in his letter to his ex-wife that his mother and aunt had been abusive and it was no wonder he was the way he was with females.*

As Millie was starting to understand, abuse may be in the past but its affliction persists through a lifetime.

> *It just seems that many people knew about his behavior but overlooked it like it wasn't real. He got fired from his job when it happened but then they put him in another department where there were no children but he had free access to the Internet and preyed on women. He acted as if it was normal behavior and believed the ten-year-old girl*

was consensual because she went to him when he asked her for a hug.

When Millie was a child, grandmothers were living under one roof with family and several generations of their relatives in the same community. "Aunties," close older women who watched over neighboring children, were no longer around as they began leaving for jobs or school. Grandchildren began missing time with grandparents telling them stories that lit their imagination and passed on traditional wisdoms. Community members began turning to offices of child or social services for food stamps and assistance instead of turning to each other.

Their role as women began changing as "forward thinking" pushed the community with messages telling them if they were not like men, their gifts were not enough. A feminist movement promoted thinking about self and being independent from the men. But the women's teachings told them they are to be in balanced responsibilities with the men. The story of Adam and Eve holds the significance of women's influence to hold up God. If she's not centered, she can topple the entire sphere of a man's life.

Was it not because of marriages like these that Solomon, king of Israel, sinned? Among the many nations there was no king like him. He was loved by his God, and God made him king over all Israel, but even he was led into sin by foreign women (Neh 13:26).

Man and woman are held responsible together to respond to the call on each of their lives.

When a man or woman wrongs another in any way and so is unfaithful to the Lord, that person is guilty (Num 5:6).

The gifts of the Spirit are given to both men and women who are His servants.

Even on my servants, both men and women, I will pour out my Spirit in those days, and they will prophesy (Acts 2:18).

The Great Law defines this peace as a set of actions that promote Creator's health and caring. The men of each clan keep a fire burning, ready to hold a discussion whenever it's necessary. The same council is given to the women of each clan to talk about the needs of the families and their community. They bring these

Shadows

concerns to the *roiane* at the council meetings where their fires unite into a general council fire.

It would harmonize with the reflection of Jesus in a new covenant calling from the east, the north, west, and south. He calls us from our sickness, our storm tossed winds of despair, from hunger and addictions; he calls us from our wanderings through vales of grief, calling to join together as we learn from each other.

The ailing waters are bringing youth together to focus on environmental issues. Knowledge is shared to preserve trees against invasive species. Mining is protested in solidarity. But the question of female and male identity is being left to social media or religious organizations that promote the thought that there is no difference between boys and girls.

Native women are identifying the resources in the community, the persons with skills to promote their language, support youth in learning heritage, and work with survivors of residential schools who had no chance to learn emotional bonding in the harshly structured institutions.

They remembered their grandparents, how they crafted cradleboards that provided security for a child and sang softly in comforting words. They considered rites of passage that reaffirm relationship between mother and daughter that today could uphold a girl through the vulnerable years of middle school, high school, and college, imparting to her that through her the people will survive. They were stepping out onto unknown waters as they sought elders to speak about how traditions could apply to today's problems.

A night when Jesus showed his disciples a new lesson, he saw his disciples out in the middle of a lake struggling against the wind and waves. They struggled through the night. When dawn came, Jesus walked out across the water toward them. He was from above, a concept in indigenous tradition that holds awareness of life's source in Sky World.

Mark, realizing the importance of this story, recorded it in Mark 6:45–52. As Jesus stepped onto the water they saw this was

Journey to the Edge of the Woods

the God of Creation. Jesus understands the storm we are in and comes for us.

For victims of sexual abuse, the cry, "Am I to be nothing more than this pain," recognizes the loss of God's expression created in us as male and female bearers of his image. Jeremiah asked, is there no physician? Is there no one who will bring the Lord into our storm? Millie walked along the path awakening to her Creator's presence, seeing his provision through the shadows of her fears, positioning herself to hear him. The disciples in the storm-tossed sea were not blamed for getting caught in a storm. There are storms even where the Lord sends us, bringing us through shadows where we never intended to go in order to change within us what we cannot do for ourselves.

The bible calls this grace.

My sacrifice, O God, is a broken spirit; a broken and contrite heart you, God, will not despise (Ps 51:17).

A person is brought into unimaginable aloneness before healing begins. There is nothing but the pain spreading within them. It is the prayer most spoken in the bible—the cry for God's mercy, longing for him to sustain us. The path is plagued by memories. Millie wondered how we can know that our Creator will accept us. The song her ancestors had sung along the path, the mournful cry from their heart to remember the instructions of God were because of the compassion bringing forgiveness that stopped the warfare in her land. Millie wondered, is there anyone she can go to with this brokenness. How do we wash it away?

As the deer pants for streams of water, so my soul pants for you, my God. My soul thirsts for God, for the living God. When can I go and meet with God? (Ps 42:1–2).

It is in this space of pain that we first invite Jesus into, not yet faith enough to invite him to be Lord of all parts of our life. By hearing the hope within the tears, Peacemaker formed a friendship with Aiionwatha that led to partnering to bring a new constitution that reverberated down through the centuries. As he gathered the first leaders by Onondaga Lake, he planted the *skarenheseh-gowah*, a white pine tree, as an evergreen covenant, the symbol of

Shadows

this sheltering peace. He explained that the roots of the Tree of Peace spread out in every direction and are called The Great White Roots. If any person or nation follows the roots to the tree, they are welcomed to find shelter if their minds respect the ways of peace.

The organization of the Great Law was so influential that envoys from Maryland, Pennsylvania, and Virginia met with delegates of the Six Nations in the early 1740s and discussed this form of governance. Canassatego, an Onondaga *roiane*, advised:

> Our wise forefathers established a union and amity between the [original] Five Nations. This has made us formidable. This has given us great weight and authority with our neighboring Nations. We are a powerful Confederacy and by your observing the same methods our wise forefathers have taken you will acquire much strength and power; therefore, whatever befalls you, do not fall out with one another.[3]

Inspired, Ben Franklin took an ember of their fire and drafted the "We the People" preamble of a constitution that would light a fire for a new nation, a contribution to the US Constitution acknowledged by the 100th Congress in a 1988 resolution.

During the bitter cold of European's first winters on the land, Haudenosaunee women gathered plants and herbs to cure the newcomers of scurvy. Modern medicine would come to list more than two hundred plants in its pharmacopoeia learned from American Indians. Health providers would begin to emphasize the connection between the spirit and physical health mirroring the practice of indigenous peoples.

Ideas in science would draw on their knowledge of astronomy and ecology. It would take centuries before science caught on to the meaning of their oral tradition—all life is interdependent. Foods of the American Indians originated more than 70 percent of the foods nourishing the world today. They had domesticated more than a 150 varieties of corn, species of beans, potatoes, squash, peppers, sunflowers, peanuts, wild rice, cranberries, and maple syrup.

3. Franklin, "Excerpts from Speeches by Canassatego."

Journey to the Edge of the Woods

America took on this knowledge to fit to their culture just as the words of Jesus are brought in to fit the peoples of the world in their own situations.

Today the concerns of distressed families transcend political and cultural differences. Their helplessness in the face of darkening wounds is the pain where God is invited to stand. Out of this pain, new relationships are weaving across cultures seeking to comfort and strengthen each other. *Tetewatén:ro tánon ska'nikón:ra kén hak* ("Let us be partners and use one mind"). Bringing the women of Akwesasne together with the non-native organizations speaking about domestic violence, visiting with child abuse agencies for resources, and forming cooperative efforts with justice systems is a continued cultural exchange that began centuries ago as God moves us toward understanding we are different parts of one body.

On that day there will be one Lord, and his name the only name (Zech 14:9).

The Haudenosaunee never surrendered their right to govern themselves. The women are vital to this. Not only do they bring the voice of the families to work with the leaders in decisions for the people, they are teaching among the young and the old protecting the knowledge of their heritage for generations yet to be born.

A shared history binds these women. Networks connecting solutions began circling the earth. Women were remembering. As they spoke, Millie looked back to what their grandmothers knew of God's unchanging ways.

2

The Woods Edge

I have so much anger and I had worked years to deal with my own past issues. I think my "obsession" with these people goes back to being abused myself . . . telling people about it and not having them listen. I don't remember when it started when I was a little girl. It just seemed to happen often when we were alone in the house. Sometimes others were home but he would corner me in one of the bedrooms and threaten to beat me up if I didn't let him touch me. That was almost a typical day for me. He was only a year older than me but I used to be a skinny, gawky kid. He was bigger and heavier and sometimes it would start with him actually being nice to me. I guess to avoid a beating it was easier for me to just let him. We were little kids but this was happening all too often. Sometimes he would corner me in one of the bedrooms of the house and begin by taunting me, calling me names, and sometimes I would fight back physically. I was only a little girl of three as far back as I can remember that my brother was doing things to me sexually. It made me feel sick and dirty and I knew it wasn't right. It didn't feel right but more often than not it seemed better to just give in so I could avoid getting beat up. The odd times I would manage to fight back I remember being able to put him in a head lock that he couldn't squirm out of. He would continue to punch me with his free hand but I would hold onto him with my arm clamped around his head, I suppose from the strength derived from the fear I felt.

—Millie

Millie was beautiful and friendly. Everywhere she went, she was known for her hard work and her quiet spirit. Yet she was deeply wounded in the way of Naomi's spirit, faint from losing home, family, and all that was secure causing her to think "the Lord's hand has turned against me!" (Ruth 1:13).

Naomi means "pleasant" but she called herself Mara, "bitter." She was a foreigner in Moab, a country hostile to her homeland of Judah. Her husband and both her grown sons had died, leaving her penniless and she decided to return to her village. Her daughter-in-law Ruth was a pagan, a Gentile, a childless widow, but would not leave Ruth. Together they journeyed back to Bethlehem where family and friends looked at her grief-stricken face astonished, asking "Can this be Naomi?"

Ruth, "lovely friend," followed the older woman's advice and married Boaz, a kinsman with responsibility to redeem Naomi. Boaz and Ruth had a son, Obed, an ancestor of Jesus. Naomi was no longer bitter. Mara, a derivative of myrrh, was seen for the healing medicine the bitter plant brought to treat wounds. A grandmother now, she spent her days caring for her grandson and family.

Kinsman redemption in the Hebrew culture became the symbol of the Redeemer who would come seeking sisters who act on faith as Ruth did toward Naomi even when there was no answer in sight. It was this trait of trusting in a higher plan that the Lord finds in his people during times of sorrow's waiting. A thousand years after Boaz and Ruth lived, their descendants, Mary and Joseph, would see the Messiah birthed on Naomi's ancestral land.

How do we become this place that God can reside?

The Woods Edge

I remember going to school and always feeling like the outcast. I wondered what would people think if they knew what was happening in my house, my home.

"Walk in the light as he is in the light" (1 John 1:7) does not mean that we'll ever live perfectly. It's a call to be honest with ourselves and others, to bring our problems to God openly and not pretend that we are always okay. So often, people assume that becoming a Christian means we are now spiritually healthy. There are no more emotional problems. We pin on a smile and hold back the process God has designed to bring about as we care for the wounded.

But David tells us in Psalm 32: "Then I acknowledged my sin to you and did not cover up my iniquity" (v. 5). When David showed his heart, it opened the door for God to come near to "surround me with songs of deliverance" (v. 7).

Jesus could hear this single heart cry even in the thronging noise of a crowd, the prayer agony of a broken life. The church's first appearance to the native people telling them they were bad, they were wrong, they must convert to be like white people has planted a perception of dismissing sorrow, insisting spirituality meant acting as if we are without pain.

Yet it is from that pain that God is building his church.

The women's movement began with pain. It didn't begin as a move to become better than or even the same as men. It began because of domestic violence and child abuse. Women were being harmed and had nowhere to turn. They had no voice. Considerable social and economic strides since then have changed women's lives but with this came the question of women's role in the community. The issue is debated in churches and roles are given definition, but what of God's balance that between man and woman?

Seeing how other teachings lead people away from God's instructions, Jeremiah said it was only a commotion that could not save them.

Surely the idolatrous commotion on the hills and mountains is a deception; surely in the Lord our God is the salvation of Israel (Jer 3:23).

Journey to the Edge of the Woods

The prophet Isaiah lamented the way youth told elders to change to accommodate them instead of leadership guiding the standards.

Youths oppress my people, women rule over them. My people, your guides lead you astray; they turn you from the path (Isa 3:12).

Women now attempt suicide at higher rates than men. They seek out health professionals nearly twice as often as males do. Studies report that from the age of twelve and up, they are more prone to depression. Rape has become a concern day to day. They carry worries their ancestors rarely thought about. And now their numbers are representing more of the prison population, rising 646 percent between 1980 and 2010, according to The Sentencing Project: Research and Advocacy for Reform.

Nearly all of these despairing women were sexually or physically violated in their youth. In Indian country women and children suffer acts of abuse statistically higher than anyone else. In 2007, 14.2 in 1,000 native children were assaulted emotionally or physically compared to 9.1 non-native children, according to the Native American Children's Alliance. The Indian Law Resource Center found Indian women are 2.5 times more likely to be assaulted and more than twice as likely to be stalked than other women in this country. One in three native women will be raped and six in ten will be physically harmed. Murder of native women is ten times the national average in some communities.

The distinction comes with a history of internalized trauma. Thousands of children from their communities were taken away and placed in boarding schools during the late 1800s. Years of loneliness, punishments for speaking their own language, and a legacy of emotional, physical, and sexual abuse left them devoid of emotional bonding. More children were removed under the Indian Adoption Project from 1958 until 1967, returning to their communities as adults without any concept of family or culture. In Canada, 150,000 children were carried away, some to die under harsh living conditions, others to survive with anger.

Shattering experiences seeded distrust of organized religion, entwining roots of despair throughout their communities.

Churches on reservations may be decorated with native symbols, feathers, baskets, and a dark-skinned Jesus, but haven't reached the traditional elders who live each day in communion with God whose presence is everywhere.

"Our people have heard about Jesus but they have heard wrongly," said native Pastor Thomas McDonald at Church of the Great Peace Native Fellowship in Ohio. "They have heard about churchianity, not about Jesus Christ. Churchianity is the enemy of the message of Christ. Once they really know who Jesus is they will believe. I have seen the true power of Jesus Christ in the native world to bring healing, wholeness, happiness, love, peace, power, and a good mind."

It's about the way we do it. In Phil 4:5 Paul tells us, "Let your gentleness be evident to all." King James translates the original word for gentleness as "moderate," like weather that is within boundaries. ASV uses the word "reasonableness." AMP translates it as unselfishness (your considerateness, your forbearing spirit). It means conscious control, a characteristic that Christ had of listening and discovering what matters to each person.

Indian nations lived feeling the pulse of creation in their own heartbeat, knowing all members of creation are needed. Every hunt that brought in food for the community was done with giving thanks to the prey for its sacrifice to their people. Talking with God was an everyday practice, not a proselytizing that was contained inside one building. Hundreds of Indian nations coexisted in their diverse customs while sharing the belief that the land belonged to one Creator.

Jeremiah mourned what God was mourning when he saw the desperate state of the daughter of God's people. He named it: "the whole head is sick, and the whole heart faint." Women are sexual objects at younger ages, cared about only for how they can make someone else feel, bereft of shelter for their heart, abortions leaving them so uncared for that a new life cannot be welcomed, media messages that focus on outward image, and separated from elders who can teach about consequence. Violent behavior among girls is rising. The Center for Disease Control reported suicide among preteens and young girls in America spiked 76 percent in the twenty-first century.[1] Children who once played freely began knowing fear of their own neighborhood as the darkness of abuse spread through the houses.

They wonder in silence, is Creator disappointed in me.

> *My mom was pretty much abandoned by her own parents who were heavy drinkers and she and her siblings ended up being taken to the Thomas Indian School on the Seneca territory, Cattaragus reservation. When she came out and came back to the rez she met my dad and they both began a life together of drinking and having a family in between. My father died on the same day as my fifteen year old brother, who got killed in a car wreck. He was driving.*

Growing up Millie smoothed down her clothes, walked out her front door, and pretended she was fine. She sat in classrooms with friends and pretended to smile. Inside her mind she smoldered with pain the adults around her did not notice.

> *So my life was just that. Being raised by a mother who instead of trying to make life better for her kids than the upbringing she had, made sure we were going to feel the same pain she did. I was ashamed of how we lived never having enough food and having a mother who was drunk a lot of the time. This left it open for my brother to begin abusing me physically and sexually.*

Millie walked through life wishing someone were happy she had been born. Where was her welcome? Her unseen tears ached for her Creator to remember her, to find her, not forgotten, and define how she matters. Without that, it was a desolate landscape, the birdsong leaving the land, chirps of chipmunks fell silent sleeping underground, foliage had fallen from the trees and she was alone without song.

> *I was the last baby born in the family and was told I was an accident. My mother would say things to me like I had*

---

1. "Teenage American Girls."

> no personality, I wasn't pretty, and no man would probably ever want me. Even though I told myself I didn't need a man, deep down I ached to have someone care for me like the unconditional love I'd had from my grandmother.

When I kept silent, my bones wasted away through my groaning all day long. For day and night your hand was heavy on me; my strength was sapped as in the heat of summer (Ps 32:3–4).

When Jeremiah spoke of balm, he referred to its source as a rare evergreen tree, spreading its branches in full sunlight on a hill beyond the Jordan River, waiting for its sweet fragrant oils to be needed, offering balm for healing wounds. Yet even when we know of the balm, there are struggles we each bring up the hill where the physician waits for our approach. There is our past, our childhood, words said to us, our disappointments, wrongs done to us, the shame of our own wrong doing all preventing the openness God longs to have with us. The shame even of those called to the promised land had burdened the children of Israel wandering through the wilderness, passing it onto generations until it was lifted by an act only God could bring. Canopied by branches, through shadowing doubts and discouragements, wearied by so many struggles inside her, Millie arrived at the edge of the woods. She stepped into sunlight where she met with other women who were like the field of wildflowers, each a gift, together strengthening each other's growth, providing sustenance for the many lives of birds and butterflies evolving alongside them.

The meadow resonates with God's promise. "I will turn the desert into pools of water, and the parched ground into springs. I will put in the desert the cedar and the acacia, the myrtle and the olive. I will set junipers in the wasteland, the fir and the cypress together" (Isa 41:18–19).

The heart of God is known most clearly in the desperate life. There was Mary Magdalene who Jesus saw surrounded by accusing persons wanting to see her punished for having relations with too many men. "Who among you is without sin, cast the first stone," Jesus said, sending her accusers away in shame. He didn't berate her for all the wrongs she'd committed. She didn't need to be told. We are told how he saw a woman who had lost her sense of value to God. This touched Mary so deeply that when he died, she was there. After he was buried, she was lost without his promise. Sleepless, she went to the tomb just to be near him.

Mary was among the first who Jesus appeared to when God resurrected him from the grave. When she saw him she wept, overcome with relief, with joy, with all the sorrow of missing him. Even then he accepted her; he did not tell her to stop being so emotional. The compassion Jesus carried was sent from God to women who were broken. He'd gone to the Samaritan woman, a woman who had failed with five husbands and was with yet another man when she met Jesus at a well. He saw in her a woman whose heart must have shattered with all the relationships that failed to find her love, leaving her so alone. "Drink of the living waters," he told her.

Forget the former things; do not dwell on the past. See I am doing a new thing! Now it springs up; do you not perceive it? I am making a way in the desert and streams in the wasteland. The wild animals honor me, the jackals and the owls, because I provide water in the desert and streams in the wasteland to give drink to my people, my chosen, the people I formed for myself that they may proclaim my praise (Isa 43:18–21).

To a believer, there is purpose in the hardships that happen.

Mary and the Samaritan woman would tell the story of the Lord speaking to their heart for the rest of their lives. He is risen. He is real. They would have had a profound message for other women who had been abused or had misused their womanhood. These women became fragrance in the meadows. The woods edge grows from such diversity, a place of both comfort and sorrow. A community of fresh raspberries and gooseberries grows here with wild geranium and orchids, and medicinal plants of joe pye, clover, horsetail, and cohosh. Each member gives places to bees and butterflies to work continuance of their gifts. Birds come and spread the seeds.

"Why then is not the health of the daughter of my people recovered?"

Thom McDonald spoke about his own experience, being Indian, as a pastor bringing Jesus to Native folks: "I think the entire problem is in the manner of presentation of the balm and the physician. I believe that most church people do not understand the real spiritual healing power of Jesus Christ," Dr. McDonald said. "Too many take the consumer approach of what can Jesus do for me not what can I do for you. There is a superficial mentality where we pick and choose what God can do for us not what we can do for God. Far too many Christians do not identify with the Cross of Christ, the love and self-sacrifice involved in truly serving instead of being served. Their idea of reaching out is discussion groups, inviting a native speaker for a Sunday, going on mission vacations, rushing into reserves to 'help' native people. But, they do not cross their denominational barriers or offer adequate financial support to real native pastors who are there truly helping their people. They are too often on instruct mode."

In the meantime, the people perish.

There are times the physician may delay bringing the balm as a person is deepened through their situation.

Humble yourselves, therefore, under God's mighty hand, that he may lift you up in due time (1 Pet 5:6).

Abraham had to wait twenty-five years for a son. Joseph waited two years in prison for deliverance. David waited seven years to sit on the throne. It was years Paul waited from his first encounter with Jesus before the rise of his ministry.

It is "through faith and patience that we inherit the promises."

For the revelation awaits an appointed time; it speaks of the end and will not prove false. Though it linger, wait for it; it will certainly come and will not delay (Hab 2:3).

At times the hindrance may be in relationship even when the physician is here.

"Concerning the brokenness, there was a very grave sin committed long ago and perpetuated through racist attitudes and actions throughout the generations," Dr. McDonald explained. "There are many types of justice but many feel that justice can never be done unless the continent is returned to its rightful owners.

Journey to the Edge of the Woods

When you are living in poverty or addiction or bitterness on a reserve, the last thing you want is for any non-native apologizing for killing your ancestors, breaking up your family, and sending your children to a residential school, destroying your way of life, discriminating against you, and then getting in their car and going back home to suburbia or wherever they live. Reconciliation may be more for the non-native people than the native people in that way."

The conscience of the non-native is salved but the native person is angered. Dr. McDonald, a Métis Indian, pointed out how the many tribes in North America had always had a practice of receiving a messenger in the spirit of trusting Creator to send words. These days, he said, "inquiring questions and new-agers pacing around like cultural vampires trying to learn native secrets alienates many native people."

A member of the Mohawk Nation explained the perception from Indian Country, "Attitudes regarding native history can be chalked up to plain and simple ignorance, plus a total lack of interest. None of this is taught in schools . . . vast land loss, government manipulations, three-hundred-plus broken treaties, millions of native deaths between 1492 and 1900, Indian slaves, and a whole lot of horrible things since 1492, not to mention the lies about the native people and culture. My father use to say, 'It soothes conscience to cast mud upon the character of a people you have wronged.' Centuries of this produces people with huge, far-reaching ignorance. Right down to the simple thing that a lot of whites can't understand why the use of Indians as mascots isn't nice, it's uncomfortable, it's insulting, and it makes Indians into cartoons."

He went on to say that schools are changing, but not fast enough or thoroughly enough. "We tried to add to the education with the curriculum guide and the state's schools, but were thwarted by certain academics, and the state didn't have enough guts to keep the native view. They backed off, apparently leaving the changes to another time, if ever."

The Woods Edge

In 1987 representatives of the State Education Department met with Haudenosaunee members, including Jake Swamp, Leon Shenandoah, Bernard Parker, Leo Henry, Doug-George Kanentiio, John Kahionhes Fadden, and others. All were in agreement that there were areas of school curriculum that needed work and they were ready to compile a supplement. A 400-page guide for schools, *Haudenosaunee: Past, Present, and Future: a Social Studies Resource Guide* was drafted.[2] The SED solicited evaluations from some thirty experts, including anthropologists, historians, and schoolteachers.

Twenty-five thought the curriculum guide was positive. Five of the reviews were negative. The state dismissed the curriculum on the basis of these five who claimed the Haudenosaunee did not align with what scholars had decided about them, despite the scholars never including the input of any Indian in their research.

In his 2014 PhD dissertation, "The Haudenosaunee and the Trolls Under the Bridge: Digging Into the Culture of 'Iroquoianist' Studies,"[3] at Binghamton University, Dr. Brian Broadrose concluded the relationship is "fraught with hostility and inequality" because "rationalizations perpetuate the notion that American Indians are inherently different from non-natives."

"The group of Iroquoianist scholars consistently minimize the role of the Haudenosaunee in their own Euroamerican culture while overstating the influence of *civilized* whites upon the Haudenosaunee," he says.

Dr. Broadrose based his thesis on the question, What really has changed since the nineteenth century? "The answer is that such differences are in appearance only, not in substance," he said. "The concern is with appearance and not content."

Some, he said, are concerned with appearing as a defender of American Indian rights. But behind the scenes they assume that westernized thinking is intended to bring the "poor Indian" their knowledge. Others, resembling church movements, go into Indian

---

2. Fadden, *Haudenosaunee: Past, Present, Future*.
3. Broadrose, "Haudenosaunee and the Trolls Under the Bridge."

country only to "convert" those who are already disconnected from their traditional heritage.

Dr. Broadrose grew up away from the traditions of his Seneca people and is of mixed descent. He learned through his research how non-traditional Indians can appropriate the symbolism of the Confederacy and speak for all Haudenosaunee, even where they lacked knowledge and practices.

"There has been a mighty struggle amongst Indians like myself," he said. "We all have that shell-shocked gaze, we all struggle with our identity of being mixed blood, ethnic Indians, urban Indians, or lost boys and we all search for the thread of connection that we hope will lead us back home."

He conceptualizes the ideal relationship between scholars and natives as the Two-Row Wampum Belt that the ancestors of both had agreed to hundreds of years ago. Separate but equal, with friendship, one of the three rows of beads that bind the two vessels traveling the river of life. When we see the river of life as Jesus, the living water, we see each people drawn under the sovereign Spirit of the Lord, singing songs of their own language, understanding the water in their own heritage.

"It means native people want non-natives to stop speaking of us in the past tense, making racist jokes, being patronizing, being fixated on native regalia and asking insensitive questions, all the while being on the verge of resorting back to their ancestor's techniques of bringing out the Army if we are becoming too 'out of control' yet all the while playing the Patriotic American card with us," Dr. McDonald said.

Churches are seeking ways to take on these concerns.

"Enact a new practice," Dr. Broadrose said. "It is my opinion, for what it is worth, this is the only sensible, real way to bring about positive change."

In the way Peacemaker modeled, many distrusting people were brought to turn their eyes onto one message and trusting, if not each other, the message. This sustained them in the century when they were surrounded by battles between the English and French, and the years when disease decimated their communities.

The Woods Edge

The law gave a way to work with others toward cleaning the river when industrial pollution destroyed their way of life. It showed them diplomacy to use in the courtrooms, halls of state capitals, and on the international stage.

Another message would follow, "by so much more Jesus has become a surety of a better covenant" (Heb 7:22). He is consecrated, "a priest forever."

Transitioning from warfare that fights to possess the land to occupying another people's land, a centurion in Israel sent elders of the Jews to Jesus when one of his valued servants fell ill. Even in this time of hostility the elders said of him, "he loves our nation." He loved their faith system. He knew their concerns, their community, and had established a relationship of respect by the time he went to the elders. He honored the protocol of Jews not entering a Gentile's house and asked only that Jesus pray for the child. In Luke 7:9 Jesus said, "I tell you, I have not found such great faith even in Israel."

Those called to intercede in Indian country must wade not only through the history of those who went before, but also more religions and alternative views than there has ever been in the history of the world. How are we distinguished when we walk along side someone in pain? Who are the Peacemakers who sit down beside someone or the Aiionwathas whose own heartbreak now sings to the wounded?

The custom was for the Haudenosaunee people to light a fire for the smoke to signal those in the village their arrival at the woods edge. A group comes out to meet them and says, "Let us refresh you. We are grateful that you arrived safely." They take soft deerskin to symbolically wipe tears from their eyes so again "you are able to see beauty and that we care about you." They take a soft eagle feather and brush dust out of their ears "so you can hear the compassion around you." There is no theoretical analysis of why they are weary and suffering. There is a cleansing through acknowledgment that every human soul needs to transform their mind from sorrows.

Cool spring water is given to drink to refresh "so you can speak and eat again because dust settles in the throat too." These words came from the suffering of Aiionwatha when he sat in loneliness at the lakeside. They were used in the process of forgiving each other at a time the people were unable to find unity.

In it is thankfulness that God is with us.

The fire that sent smoke rising to heaven had nearly been extinguished. As the women looked back to what that fire brought their people, they found that the precepts that govern life do not change. God's instructions do not alter. Every person they see will one day be gathered to their fathers. Every neighbor they encounter will be wounded in some way. In Indian country it is the community members who are the responders. In a world of intensifying tears, they looked back to what their ancestors knew.

For the time will come when people will not put up with sound doctrine. Instead, to suit their own desires, they will gather around them a great number of teachers to say what their itching ears want to hear. They will turn their ears away from the truth and turn aside to myths. But you, keep your head in all situations, endure hardship, do the work of an evangelist, discharge all the duties of your ministry (2 Tim 4:3–5).

They defined for themselves their need to first become whole.

The agreed upon Two Row covenant had extended from the precepts that governed the communities. The concept of equal respect was between wife and husband as a way of life, between parents and children that acknowledged each hold valued responsibilities. It's foundational to the principles of Native philosophy and continues to be extended today.

In early springtime 2012 the Mohawk women traveled to New York City to participate in a panel discussion at the National Museum of the American Indian. The public event, "Native Women's Empowerment: A Mohawk Reflection," shared ways they apply ancient responsibilities to today's world. Present from Akwesasne were Louise McDonald and Sherrill Elizabeth Tekatsitsiakwa "Katsi" Cook and from the Tyendinaga Mohawk reserve, Mary Anne Spencer.

The Woods Edge

Mary Ann is the program elder for a Master of Social Work Program at Sir Wilfrid Laurier University near Toronto. Teaching the indigenous holistic approach, she said the entire community is included in considerations needed to restore an individual from the problems left by colonizing.

Katsi is an elder and director of First Environment Collaborative, a reproductive health and justice program, and director of Running Strong for American Indian Youth. Until the 1950s grandmothers and older female relatives were midwives tending young mothers. The fishermen out on the rushing river would bring in plentiful fish to people gathered on the shores waiting to prepare a picnic. Children learned the water's currents and swam in summertime. The warm sun, the backyard gardens, the places where berries grew abundantly supported a trusted environment that would be mourned when it was lost to the toxins from industry.

Katsi's presentation, "You are Creation," relates how the environment around us and personal choices validate the midwives advice on how to behave during pregnancy. The session, "Protocols of Peace: Native Condolence and the Good Mind in Northern America," stressed the need for the Edge of the Wood Ceremony to lift burdens of stress and suffering so they are not integrated into the body to become disease.

"A good place to start is by acknowledging their journeys," Katsi said.

It became evident that the dignity of man and woman as a mortal creation of the eternal God was being lost under abusive behaviors becoming accepted as normal day occurrences. A system of rationalizations broke the cord and the integrity of family was unraveling. God, who created his image to yearn toward coming together as one, was witnessing man and woman in sexual brokenness from uncaring relationships. Present day teachings pointed inward for solutions, thinking everything we need to become fulfilled and stronger than the wounds is within our own self-empowerment.

Looking inward, Millie found what we do find—unbearable hurt, deep loneliness, and helplessness in the face of horrible abuse that grows strong in a society forgetting God.

My people have committed two sins: They have forsaken me, the spring of living water, and have dug their own cisterns, broken cisterns that cannot hold water (Jer 2:13).

When he saw this happening to his people, Jeremiah gave God's warning of what it would bring.

I will bring an end to the sounds of joy and gladness and to the voices of bride and bridegroom in the towns of Judah and the streets of Jerusalem, for the land will become desolate (Jer 7:34).

The language of heaven holds communion with God, able to invite the presence of Jesus without one gift becoming another in any land, but each being the gift God intended for the whole.

Entering a circle of native women, Millie is embraced by the familiar rhythm of a drum, the scent of sage that tells her she is one of their own. As the people are coming together through sharing their stories, it is the comfort of understanding that is rekindling trust. Millie could not choose the past her family had created in her, but here where each flower and each tribe of grasses carried on its assignment from God, she could find a welcome in the sun that returns each morning, the earth beneath her feet that would bring new life and sustenance, the sheltering trees that remind of the Tree of Life in the sky world. A welcome that remains present even when there is nothing and no one who understands or brings justice.

Like Aiionwatha, Millie's eyes were clouded with grief and she hadn't been able to see the beauty still in the world all around her and in herself. She hadn't been able to hear the voices that assure her of life, or to be able to speak again and express herself.

She could see the power of Creator's goodness and believe in her own uniqueness as a created being, but she didn't yet have her identity given a woman from the Lord. Who would bring her this balm? Who would tell her of the ark of salvation so near waiting for her to come into it, a redeemer watching, understanding, saying, "Come, I am here, wanting your heart to trust me so I can dwell within you." To help us understand, Jesus used the allegory of being a vine with many branches, all growing from the same source of water. We come together in relationship because of being rooted in the same water, but the branch may differ in its growth and in its purpose.

When Peacemaker came to Aiionwatha, where he sat destroyed by all that had befallen him, he did not offer advice to Aiionwatha. Moved by the sorrow he witnessed, he entered into suffering with him. He picked up the wampum strings that Aiionwatha had made and spoke words that reflected the pain scorching Aiionwatha's mind. Aiionwatha felt known. He had been heard.

Peacemaker's action told Aiionwatha that he believed in him. He saw purpose in Aiionwatha's life and knew he had a future. In the Spirit of God, he had come to the brokenhearted to build a new architecture, the people of the longhouse. Millie's childhood suffering was never consoled. She grew up bringing a broken heart into her marriage.

> *My work takes me to many communities. This is how B and I got together. When I got to Ontario the last week of August, he sent his first email that was flirty. A few lines that asked me, "Are you single these days?" The first few weeks in September we were emailing back and forth and he sent me an email saying, "I'm crushin' on you." I asked if it was some kind of a joke and he said no, it was for real and that he'd had a crush on me for a long time. He said he was first attracted to me when I spoke to him at an event more than ten years ago. In the beginning I said no. He asked me for a friends-with-benefits kind of thing and I outright said no.*

He persisted and one day when he asked to meet her for lunch, Millie went.

> *I admit I was attracted to him and very flattered when he said he liked me. A visit in October and meeting him in person again after he'd said he was "crushin" on me had me thinking very differently about him.*

Journey to the Edge of the Woods

She tried to speak with her husband about her feelings of loneliness, her ache to be cherished. She lacked something, she said, she was empty inside, but his response was to tell her he'd been happy in the marriage and whatever the problem is, it was in her.

To find acceptance that was not dependant on someone else's definition whether it's a man or society, Millie came into the circle where she could be truly known. The circle formed in 2009 when the Konon:kwe Council came together to "reconstruct the power of our origins through collaborative approaches to the care, empowerment, and transformation of a traumatized indigenous community." The stories of being raped as a little girl and of suicidal thoughts brought tears. In the sanctity of concern for each other they developed ways for girls to speak openly, circles of men to guide the boys, feelings of hope as they sang social songs and remembered the supports around them.

In community, the presence of elders is prominent. They have lived a long time through many struggles, understanding the process of grief. The endearment "Tóta" is used to address all elders as grandmothers and grandfathers throughout the community. Elders are the bridge to ancient values that guided the people. As new influences encroached around them, elders remind of where we come from and how we belong.

The people went to the elders to restore their original language. There is an annual Native Film Festival in June done all in language to showcase the resources. Celebrated every year, Aboriginal Language Day is hosted by a community-wide show with guests from other language programs locally and at other Mohawk territories. The bi-annual Sweetgrass Language Conference brings together people from across the continent to Belleville, Ontario near the Tyendinaga Mohawk Territory.

Contained in the words is their covenant relationship to each other, the voice of their grandparents, the land of their ancestors, and Creator who sustains all life.

Forty years of fluoride emissions pouring into their territory, the chemicals settling in the river, and the processed foods that replaced the land's bounty caused new diseases that necessitated other medical care. Many of the people go for treatment to doctors as well as continuing traditional healing. In recent years in the spirit of the Two Row knowledge of health began being exchanged to help both peoples to minister to the connection between mind, body, and spirit.

When the apostle Paul spoke about the need for this discipline, he was speaking about the importance of mind, body, and spirit all working in one conscious choice for God.

Therefore, since we have these promises, dear friends, let us purify ourselves from everything that contaminates body and spirit, perfecting holiness out of reverence for God (2 Cor 7:1).

Integral to the disciplined health of communities is the mother who carries her newborn infant to the longhouse to present to the entire community. She needs the support of each of their gifts. The child belongs to them too and will know he was thought of before he was born. To remind how important a child is to God's plan, Peacemaker offered instructions through the naming ceremony:

> When an infant of the Five Nations is given an Authorized Name at the Midwinter Festival or at the Ripe Corn Festival, one in the cousinhood of which the infant is a member shall be appointed a speaker. He shall then announce to the opposite cousinhood the names of the father and the mother of the child together with the clan of the mother. Then the speaker shall announce the child's name twice. The uncle of the child shall then take the child in his arms and walking up and down the room shall sing: "My head is firm, I am of the Confederacy."

The land and people will always welcome him. The men have sung over him.

> *My mother was a raging alcoholic and her son, who was her pride and joy, was beating me and molesting me and I knew she knew. Even as a little kid I knew she knew but never acknowledged it. I remember going up to my sister who was three years older than me and whispering to*

> her that he was doing things to me. I just remember her brushing it off but I had hoped if I told her she would make him stop. She would yell at him, threatening she would do something but she didn't. It continued until I was nine years old and I can remember the day I finally was able to say, Kakweni! (Enough!) I remember that day clearly like it happened only yesterday. I had come out of the bedroom leading to the kitchen and being in a small house, it was hard to avoid anyone in the downstairs part of our house. I came walking out and he came from the living room toward me with that look. A look that told me I was going to get trouble, or that he was going to ask me to pull my pants down, or that he would pull down his pants. I don't know why it was different that day. I don't know why he finally listened to my refusal but he stopped.

If she could know Jesus as someone other than the one used in the genocide and assimilation of her people, he could bring about a new objective and it could be said, as the women said to Naomi in Ruth: "Blessed be the Lord, who has not left you this day without a redeemer" (4:14).

No mother's comfort or father's assurance, left unguarded, always trying to find a way to believe in a relationship, Millie only found disappointment again and again. Missing was the passage into womanhood, the rites that marked a girl's growth and defined her with our Creator's identity. In Mohawk language, as in the Torah that structured the Hebrew people's community, there is no word for adolescence. There is childhood that is modeled to become the concerns of adulthood as they take their place among the elders. Without this secure circle around her to show her what caring looked like, Millie was beguiled by B's victimizing words.

> I saw him as a caring father who was involved with his children, something my partner didn't do. I was suddenly being told I was smart, beautiful, something my husband didn't say. I actually believed B when he said he was trapped in his relationship because of his child. That was why I couldn't seem to walk away. It really hurt to be told I was used and that he never had feelings for me, and then to discover he'd violated young girls.

The Woods Edge

The affair with B began in the spring and lasted until early October. Then he told Millie it was just a game and he'd only used her simply because he could. Millie was devastated. No comforting thoughts reached her because of her guilt in breaking her marriage covenant.

> *I was hurt and angry because B had told me that we should end things and I responded angrily but I stopped contacting him. That night as I was packing to leave for home he messaged me asking, "Are you hating me?" I shut down my computer and didn't respond. After a couple of weeks I did respond, saying I didn't hate him, that I was just hurt.*

Paralyzing pain expanded in a helpless rage, exposed and vulnerable, and she struck back. Disbelief at finding no one had stood against him when they knew what he was doing tormented, just as no one had stood for her in her childhood. She thought: *Somewhere tonight a child silently endures. A woman is being bruised. An elder is shrinking back from screaming voices. A brother is being shoved.* She discovered few protections for any of them as she learned more about B and the epidemic of abuses. She called him, accused him, blamed him, until the anger turned inward on herself.

Depression washed over her. Physically helpless as a child, emotionally helpless as an adult, she emptied into hopelessness. Time and distance did not quench the pain and guilt. Psychology gained her perspectives but did not rid the depression pulling her down. Friends assured her it was not her fault, but it did not erase the residue.

3

Through Fields of Harvest

One day in April I felt defeated. He was coming to the pow wow that summer and I felt awful about it because I had asked him not to come. I thought no matter what I do, no matter what I say, no matter who knows the horrid details about him, he was going to come out of it all without a scar. I was talking to the council to make sure they were aware of this man. He had said that his mom had molested him from the time he was eight to twelve years old and that an aunt also molested him once. He said it was no wonder why he was the way he was with women. In a letter he named four girls that he had done things to but seemed to try and justify it all. Two were ten and eleven years old.

—Millie

For you created my inmost being; you knit me together in my mother's womb (Ps 139:13).

The power of God's presence in the womb asks our responsibility to protect, nurture, and teach the knowledge of the Lord just as Eve and Adam continued even after the mistake that brought murder, lies, and violence into the world. This power was shown in the prayer of Elizabeth (Eli-sheba: "My God is generous"). Long after all hope of having a child was gone and she and her husband Zechariah were elderly, Elizabeth became pregnant with John the Baptist.

Elizabeth was an older cousin of Mary who was pregnant with Jesus at the time. Mary, under great suspicion as an unmarried woman pregnant with child, visited Elizabeth. Immediately the kinswomen recognized they were both carrying children of extraordinary destiny. The recognition was given to Zechariah too, who was struck mute in the afternoon he entered the temple to offer incense at a time his people were under Roman occupation. The angel Gabriel appeared to him and announced that his wife would have a son. Only after John was born and Zechariah agreed to his name ("God is gracious") could he speak again and rejoice with his wife. The angel told Zechariah his son would be filled with the Spirit from his conception. He would prepare a way for the Messiah.

Heightened with anticipation that God was moving on behalf of his people, Elizabeth blessed Mary.

Blessed are you among women, and blessed is the child you will bear! But why am I so favored, that the mother of my Lord should come to me? As soon as the sound of your greeting reached my ears, the baby in my womb leaped for joy. Blessed is she who has believed that the Lord would fulfill his promises to her! (Luke 1:42–45).

Sharing stories of women's experiences with the generations coming up behind us holds the wonder of God's presence, the expectation Eve had when she spoke of Seth and Elizabeth had when she spoke of her unborn child. God has a plan to fulfill.

The war against women and children is intensifying.

The world has never seen such a large population of youth as it sees today. According to the United Nations, about 40 percent of the earth's population was under the age of twenty-five in 2014. Among these are 67 million indigenous youth surrounded by challenges never before experienced. They live aware of physical abuse killing 57,000 of the world's children every year. Sexual abuse, child prostitution and pornography, neglect, emotional abuse, an estimated 246 million in child labor, others sent into trafficking, and illegal adoptions by western countries are their realities.[1]

Gathering in New York City to discuss these issues in the winter of 2013 youth representatives from countries including Australia, Canada, Finland, Peru, and Uganda looked for ways to respond. The event was "Indigenous Youth: Identity, Challenges and Hope: Articles 14, 17, 21 and 25 of the United Nations Declaration on the Rights of Indigenous Peoples."

"Indigenous youth struggle to develop and define their identities, maintain their cultures, and preserve and revitalize their languages," Shamshad Akhtar reported, Assistant Secretary-General in the UN's Department of Economic and Social Affairs.

Ms. Akhtar told the gathering a "younger generation of indigenous population can be promising for their community if their vitality and vigor is appropriately unleashed and they can transform the overall indigenous community's destiny. Youth drives idealism, creativity, entrepreneurship, and with appropriate support can help make the world a better place."

Locally women began meeting with each other. In October 2012 the Mohawk women of the Gwitch'in, Anishinabe, Kogi, and other nations from around North and South America gathered for a four-day meeting of Weaving Webs of Women's Wisdom, addressing the violence and abuse Konon:kwe Council greeted women from Lakota, Hopi, Diné, Pima, Crow, Cheyenne, with women's knowledge.

Gathered with the three hundred guests were health service directors, nurse practitioners, midwives, clan mothers, victim advocates, first responders, and police officers. They listened to each other's stories about the horror of rape, torture, and severe assaults, the majority against native women involving non-native men. Led by Bear Clan Mother Tewakierahkwa Louise McDonald, the community movement gifted braids of corn, the mother plant, to the visiting women. Among them two elder Kogi women and two

---

1. Department of Economic and Social Affairs, "Concise Report."

traditional Kogi men from northern Columbia brought a message of the struggling health of *la Madre Tierra* ("the Mother Earth") where they live in the mountains of Sierra Nevada de Santa Marta.

One of the Kogi women stepped forward and placed a small gourd in the center of the circle of women. She asked what they thought they should pay the Moon, the Sun, the Air, and the quaking inside Mother Earth for all they have given to life. Everyone placed imagined payment into the gourd in ceremonial thanks for nature's helpers. The Kogi packaged the gourd to bring it back to their mountain where their medicine people would burn it in a fire of shared prayer.

After the ceremony the women danced in their tradition of appreciation for earth. They were gathered near the St. Regis River that flows into the St. Lawrence and they spoke of the afflictions of women corresponding to the suffering of earth. Patterns in nature are being lost, they said, unable to respond as they once did.

The days of sharing began with protocols that have always governed meetings between first nations on the land, by sending a runner between the groups to ask if they came in peace. Songs of welcome were sung. Before talking began, the Edge of the Woods Ceremony was offered to refresh the weary travelers and ease stress. They gave comfort to each other as they brought the stories into the light. They took on the concerns of each other. They shared knowledge to strengthen each other. This was the language of God.

Beyond the woods edge, through the field, is the village surrounded by gardens of harvest. Given understanding from the consoling ceremony that we all are broken and struggling, Millie walked onto the narrow path leading to the village where she sought to be in community with others. She slowed under the weight of memory. Regrets of the times she had failed God made her want to turn back. Shame took the place of feeling she belonged out here in the light.

The resistance is met many times along this path. We are limited by our losses, illness, divorces, betrayals, suicides, disappointments, undependability, and all the heartache suffered all around us. We're also constrained by societal norms that shape acceptable expression of grief. Cultural protocols transformed Millie toward the community beyond yet each step brought her needing more mercy.

"He must become greater; I must become less," John said (3:30).

We visit and we talk, finding we have only what Elizabeth's son, John, had to offer. Prepare the way for the Lord. Crowds went out to John as he traveled in the Jordan Valley, desperate for consoling. They gravitated to his message: "The lamb of God that takes away the sin of the world" (John 1:29).

We have only the news of a risen priest. "For such a High Priest was fitting for us, who is holy, harmless, undefiled, separate from sinners, and has become higher than the heavens" (Heb 7:26).

The message given is too often only about His saving power of our soul after death. To a people who view "walking on" as a return to their ancestors, afterlife is not news. Saving us in the circumstances around us when the world offers no justice and no protections is a message no cultural practice can bring without God's son. It doesn't matter if the people are from the Longhouse, Medwin, Shaking House, or local church building. Women are striving for their children to be well and safe in what is becoming increasingly a spiritual warfare.

The work has not changed. In John 6:29, Jesus defined it for all time, "The work of God is this: to believe in the one he has sent." God spoke through Moses to tell the Egyptians, "Let my people go." The situation worsened for the people, who were held as slaves by the Egyptians. Pharaoh now demanded they continue making the same number of bricks but would no longer give them straw. Moses turned to God asking why this was getting worse. He was seeing his people suffer even more. He asked, why send me when it only made things worse. And God responded, "Now you will see what I will do" (Exod 6:1).

Let my people go, God again spoke through Moses. Let my people go that they may serve me. All through the book of Exodus chapters 5–8, He spoke. Let them go. They may serve me.

I will take you to be my people, and I will be your God, and you shall know that I am the Lord your God, who has brought you out from under the burdens of the Egyptians.

And God did.

The story of the Haudenosaunee is one of exodus. Brought out of a time of oppression, anger, fighting, and fear, the Haudenosaunee came into a formation of peaceful diplomacy centered in giving thanks. Brought out of centuries of injustice they came to speak on world platforms on behalf of all peoples. Brought out of the poisons that afflicted their water they formed partnerships for healthy rivers, lakes, and oceans for all peoples. Brought out of abuse of their children there is a new message of peace coming along the path Peacemaker made ready.

Early mission work into Indian country slowed by the beginning of the nineteenth century because European settlers had grown hostile toward the Indians. But as struggles to protect home and family spread among all peoples, the need to be governed by a higher law revived missions with a new consciousness.

May God arise, may his enemies be scattered (Ps 68:1).

As God's Spirit moves through the breakdown of healthy water, extinction of species, illnesses, and the cry of children, He has begun to cleanse relationship between nations through awareness of our mutual need.

Your procession, God, has come into view (Ps 68:24).

Today native pastors taking up the message of Jesus are often on the lowest end of the pay scale yet deal with people who face the toughest challenges in the shadows of massacres and extermination policies. From time to time non-native churches wanting dialogue have asked Dr. Thom McDonald how to minister to native people.

"I recommend that they support native ministry, not denomination-run churches because once again the non-native denomination is calling the shots," he said. "They want to hold endless meetings and studies on how to do it instead of opening their wallets and supporting that native pastor in a remote location who is trying to help the people. This is obstacle one. They have the money and resources but will not entrust a native pastor to do the job. They don't know the people so they can't get the job done. All they can do is go on a mission trip for one or two weeks and go back home."

Another obstacle is lack of understanding about what is traditional and what is not.

"You must know the protocol and traditions for that to happen," he said. "For me, tradition is knowing your language, the medicines, the land, your foods, your culture, and your Creator. The church is a longhouse also although in the old days there was no longhouse religion. It was simply following the path of our Creator, praying right from your heart directly to God, honoring but not worshipping His creation, not practicing witchcraft. We still do that today. Jesus taught this."

Protecting the daily, seasonal, and annual rhythms of keeping communion centers each member in times of incredible injustice to the nations. The practices perceive the need for the collective, every part of the community to be well to close gates to the echoes in Millie's mind telling her how much she failed.

Millie passed through the fields of harvest where grandmothers and young children would talk together as they gathered foods for their families. Seeds from corn, climbing beans, and squash that were given at creation are planted here.

Called the Three Sisters, they are companions planted together on a mound of soil. Corn seeds are tucked in the middle and seeds of beans and squash are alternated around the corn so the three benefit each other. Beans hold onto the corn stalks as they seek sunshine and bring nitrogen into the soil for the others. Squash spreads out, holding moisture in the ground and preventing weeds. The sisters have given the people many combinations of dishes that sustained the people through thousands of years. Corn gave husks to weave into dolls and rugs. Husks could stuff mattresses, be lit as a torch or used to wrap food for baking. Dried cobs were tossed onto fires burning to cure meat.

The Three Sisters, called *De-o-ha-ko* ("our sustainers"), are living gifts given from heaven. Drawing on their interdependent relationship that brings about more abundant growth, an outreach program was named The Three Sisters in 1996 to provide a safe home for victims of violence, sexual assault, and stalking. The St. Regis Mohawk Tribe Sexual Assault Response Team evolved to include the Three Sisters Program, the St. Regis Mohawk Tribal Police, Health Services Division, Social Services Division, the Franklin Country District Attorney's Office, and the United States Attorney's Office. Their posted message offering condolence for those who had been raped or sexually assaulted reads:

> "You are owed an apology. The community failed in its role and responsibility to keep you safe. Nothing you did or did not do caused what happened to you. No matter what, you did not deserve it. You are not to blame. For those who failed you, we are sorry and apologize for not keeping you safe."

The abuse does not have the final word on defining Millie's identity as a woman. The Three Sisters Program was there along her way to the symbol of her spiritual center, the longhouse, to remind of truths that Creator made apparent in the stories passed to each generation. It was in the creation all around whispering to her that she is a daughter of God who was harmed. The river rushing through her land could be heard in the promise.

Water will gush forth in the wilderness and streams in the desert. The burning sand will become a pool, the thirsty ground bubbling springs. In the haunts where jackals once lay, grass and reeds and papyrus will grow. And a highway will be there; it will be called the Way of Holiness. The unclean will not journey on it; it will be for those who walk in the Way (Isa 35:6–8).

Based on knowledge reminding that "the basic patterns of nature have not changed, we still live in the same areas as our ancestors, so we understand how nature works in our territories," the Whole Health Initiative began in 2000 to strengthen physical health by returning to traditional foods that maintain spiritual thanksgivings. Those with knowledge of the foods and medicinal plants in each of their regions share back and forth as in days of old, trading the resources of what the land grew each season, abundant berries in one part of the state, sassafras in another, or ash splints for basket making and harvests of backyard gardens.

Indian country has to persistently defend ecology to continue traditional farming and fishing to maintain health. To understand the integrity of their message, traditional people who are empirically still near to the natural world need to be approached with respect for how they are bound in a covenant with God and earth. Women's relationship to resources is in this covenant. Intimate knowledge of what goes on in the community, the innate ability to feel joy and bring that encouragement, stands against the hidden traumas.

Babies are again being born into the hands of their own people. Children are again growing up knowing the people who were present when they entered this world and hearing the story told of their coming.

Under the Great Law when a new child is birthed there is a welcome in the longhouse. Being a part of upholding the confederacy, the child will grow hearing the words "use good mind" many times. The concept was so pervasively understood that there was no need for prisons or enforcing many laws onto the people. The women and men supported each other in this. As they reinforced these lessons, the Konon:kwe Council hosted O'tsienhahkta (near the fire) Men's Gathering assembled with speakers from across the six nations. They spoke of how to be a leader by first proving themselves at home. This is similar to the biblical instructions for men to look up to the One who made them so that "you and your son and your grandson might fear the Lord" (Deut 6:2).

This is stewardship.

Such a man shows daughters what a man of faith looks like. Elders pass on awareness of how the young can become elegant women full of good memories or the consequences of one with the weight of regret bending her in solitary tears. The phrase "good mind" reminds each person that they hold the choice of gentle words because words walk to the creation and out to the east, the north, the west, south, and to the Creator. Retelling the stories of Peacemaker teach youth to be aware of the thoughts that resulted in the time of terrible fighting. Self-control is an appeal to a woman and a man to recognize that their sphere of influence brings tremendous attitude to the home. Good mind creates the place a child is born into.

The fourth preamble of the UN's Declaration on the Rights of Indigenous Peoples affirms that all doctrines, policies, and practices based on superiority of any one people on the basis of nationality, race, religion, ethnic or cultural differences are racist, scientifically false, legally invalid, and socially unjust.

Talk of political justifications such as the doctrine of discovery and doctrine of domination used in courts to extinguish land rights gained momentum in the two decades leading to the UN's 2012 Permanent Forum of Indigenous Issues. The Forum's Special theme was titled "The Doctrine of Discovery: Its enduring impact on indigenous peoples and the right to redress for past conquests."

The doctrines of the fifteenth century asserted authority over indigenous people by labeling them "savages," "inferior," and "uncivilized." The Forum statement said, "No other peoples in the world are pressured to have their rights extinguished."

Extinguishing the rights of people to their lands has resulted in grievous violence against indigenous women and girls, high rates of suicide, and hopelessness among young men. Meenakshi Munda, a young woman from a community in Jharkhand, traveled to New York to speak to the UN in 2012, emphasizing the importance of youth having an identity and maintaining their languages and the rich cultural wisdom. As President of the Asia Pacific Indigenous Youth Network she said, "This knowledge is intact in mother tongue. If we want to learn that, we have to learn indigenous language. Also, our oral history is intact in mother tongue, so if we want to know our own history, we have to know our own culture, our own language."

In communities the women work to promote meaningful ways existing programs and agencies can be brought to families caught in the complexities of trauma and healing. At the turn of the century the Mohawk women came together to form Ohero:kon (Under the Husk), to continue the ceremonial rite of passage that

Journey to the Edge of the Woods

guides Mohawk youth in the transformation from adolescence into adulthood in today's world. During twenty weeks of affirmation of their identity and traditional knowledge, the youth fast to prepare for contributing to the strength of their people.

As a clan mother for the Mohawk Nation Council of Chiefs, Louise McDonald is instrumental in selecting and raising the nation's leaders. As a prevention specialist for the Wholistic Health and Wellness department, she organizes the Ohero:kon to include teen relationship activities, instruction on a good life, finding a good partner and being one worth waiting for, knowledge of earth's sustenance in the forests and fields, communication skills, and star knowledge. In our world today there is also bystander training to intervene when bullying or abuse is seen. According to workers in domestic and child abuse, witnesses who stand up against it are the greatest protection for victims.

Nearly one in ten American youth fourteen to twenty-one years old reported committing an act of sexual violence at least once, revealed in a 2013 survey by the Center for Innovative Public Health Research in California and the University of New Hampshire's Crimes Against Children Research Center.[2] Surrounded by media messages of a skewed male-female relationship, sexual stereotypes, and lack of modeling the dignity of a man toward a woman, 4 percent of the national two-year survey reported attempting or committing rape.

They were not all boys. Girls are becoming perpetrators in coercion, increasing in likelihood as they grew older. The highest percentage of perpetrators was white youth from higher income families exposed daily to media images portraying women as sexual objects to be used. This empha

It is rare for perpetrators to be caught or take responsibility, leaving the victims without any sense of justice in a world that seems more and more to take these behaviors as a norm.

But one thing I do: Forgetting what is behind and straining toward what is ahead, I press on toward the goal to win the prize

---

2. Kaiser, "Sexual Violence."

for which God has called me heavenward in Christ Jesus (Phil 3:13–14).

The disciples of Jesus modeled this moving forward toward God while continuing honor for their own heritage even in days of prison and death. In native tradition honoring God means the people are to look at how each element of creation will be affected by decisions. They look to those who went before them who had insured the land, the river, and knowledge of their governance would be there for them.

When Aiionwatha lost three daughters, his grief overwhelmed him so much that he left the village and wandered in the dark forest. He came to a lake and sat at his camp, thinking about his loss. People saw his fire and came to talk with him but he was too deep in sadness to respond. He was invited into homes but when he went, his emotional state was ignored.

Aiionwatha's comfort is spoken at the Edge of the Woods Ceremony first with a wampum given because of the tears people cry. The people are saying, "We're going to take a moment to cry with you." Before they go to the village, those who journeyed through the woods reciprocate and say to those who met them, "Now let us do that for you." Then they both can continue on the path through the field leading to the community.

Blessed be the God and Father of our Lord Jesus Christ, the Father of mercies and God of all comfort, who comforts us in all our tribulation, that we may be able to comfort those who are in any trouble, with the comfort with which we ourselves are comforted by God (2 Cor 1:3–4).

That sense of deepening waters darkening around her, no one's hand reaching to grab Millie and pull her to solid ground had Millie seeking it in relationship, always disappointed, always hoping to get a different result. In meeting with the members of community, she was able to share her truths for the first time.

> *We become addicted to the people we end up with for a variety of reasons even if the relationship is not healthy for us. We need to look at the characteristics of the people we've had relationships with and to look at the pattern of*

> who we end up with. Not even examining I can see that I end up with men who are emotionally distant and preoccupied with sex. A husband with his porn, which I never viewed until I ended up with him and he led me to believe it's normal in spite of being uncomfortable with it. And B was into cybersex, which was very uncomfortable. It goes back to my being sexually abused and not knowing what is healthy and acceptable. Despite not being comfortable with it, I engaged in it because it pleased them. I'm not in any way trying to justify that my behavior was any better but only to point out that when anyone, usually men, tells me their logic in any matter, I feel as if my opinion or views are wrong.

When she was a little girl and most in need of those around her to protect her, Millie was taken advantage of by someone she knew. She was assaulted relentlessly—verbally, physically, and sexually. Instead of kind nurturing words to validate the best of her instincts, she was demeaned. Instead of physical safety, she was hurt in her own home. She didn't grow able to conceive of the beauty of union with a man. Instead she was trapped in deep loneliness, suffering from the dark balances in the world that tear down women. She wondered if she ever could recover.

Although God forgave, her nightmares echoed over and over down the corridor to her mind. Taking on the covering of Christ's righteousness does not mean the pain no longer hurts. Even Aiionwatha, having accepted his destiny to create a confederacy of peace out of the violence that had killed his own daughters must have continued to mourn their loss. A life of regret is not what God wants when he brings us to see our weakness. David in the book of 2 Samuel is brought to realize his wrong was against God when he took another man's wife. The prophet Nathan assured him that although there are consequences to our mistakes, "The Lord has taken away your sin. You are not going to die" (2 Sam 12:13).

The women of the world's nations are coming across cultures, history, and politics by presenting the hurting heart. Recognizing the need in each other, they began to cleanse from the past together. "Godly sorrow brings repentance that leads to salvation and leaves no regret, but worldly sorrow brings death" (2 Cor 7:10). The call on Peter as an apostle was brought from his sorrow after Jesus asked him one question: "Peter do you love me?" Peter answered, "Lord, you know that I love you." That's all that was needed to reinstate Peter in their relationship. He was overcome by his need for God.

Millie crossed the fields where harvests nourishing all life were designed by God who instructed Matthew to tell us to pray for those who have harmed us, "that you may be the children of your Father who is in Heaven. For he makes his sun to rise on the evil and on the good, and sends rain on the just and on the unjust" (Matt 5:45). Could hurt so damaging we remember it all our life, like Millie's mother, or scorning like her brother's, come to see the Lord's restoration?

Our resolve will never accomplish this. All man's knowledge has not redeemed the fallen world. It is uncovering the pain, helplessly empty handed, that we come to say, "we need what only you can do." In going to the fire, sending prayers to carry upward in smoke, in traditions of cleansing, is the invitation for Creator's presence to bring courage. What Aiionwatha came to understand about suffering became the most significant part of his life story. Out of it grew an ability to bring condolence to others, a light that brought about forgiveness, a unity displacing betrayals, and creation of a league that withstood centuries of every kind of oppression and influence from the world around it.

We know we are beginning to heal when we realize he has made a path for us.

Aiionwatha helped others to see the harm that happens in their vengeful minds. He affected great change when he helped them see Creator had a purpose for them. Millie had to choose how to respond to all that had happened to her. She had to choose to have her mind redeemed.

When the women gathered they returned to the foundation of who a woman is in creation. Not cut to fit political correctness or the changing tides of tolerance and ambition, but a balance to family and community by carrying the responsibility of their gifts. No one can validate this and no one can take this from them.

Yet you, Lord, are our Father. We are the clay, you are the potter; we are all the work of your hand (Isa 64:8).

> There were others. He claimed he was only around twenty and that the girls were around fourteen but she was ten years younger than him. His ex-wife said she didn't give the letter to police because she didn't know if the girls, now women, had told anyone and she was protecting them. I find this very hard to believe. She could've given the letter to police and let them decide how to handle it.

A council member sent an email asking the woman to come forward:

> It has been a long time since I talked with you regarding the violation of your daughter. At the time we spoke, I could hear the anger in your voice as you asked why nothing was done by the community. I told you honestly that I was not aware of what had happened; it had been kept quiet so well. It was only after talking to someone that I first heard about the incident. I do not know why it was ignored but now I am trying to help to bring it further to light, so that it doesn't happen again. I have talked to different decision makers and they all ask, Where is the proof? I understand now that you have significant proof; a letter handwritten by the molester. And I know that it is very sensitive since it names other victims. My wish is that this had been disclosed earlier; maybe some appointments would never have been made. We cannot go back and rectify that but we can go forward with the truth. There is a new administration now and they have pledged in their platform to provide safe measures for our children; to create a safe environment for them. I have personally talked to a few of these elected officials and I have asked for their assistance. They in turn have asked me to provide proof of any and all allegations. I am therefore requesting your help; can you provide me the letter? It can be whited-out where appropriate to protect innocent children, but the essence of the admissions is vital. What will come of this? I cannot say for certain but

I am willing to believe that awareness may save another victim. *Nya:weh* (thank you)

She never showed the letter but said if others had come forward this may not have happened to her family. Federal law has recognized child sexual abuse as maltreatment since cries from communities reached Congressional hearings in 1973. In 1989, The United Nations formed an international treaty—Convention on the Rights of the Child—that mandates the protection of the signatories' children. But the tendency remains to hide its shame.

> *It's difficult to know that this man feels no remorse for the people he hurt. He refers to accusations as ruining his life but it didn't. He's still out there at public events.*

A father of several children, B holds a position of responsibility that strengthens the ties of family and community. Many found it impossible to believe that this man had been molesting young girls aged eight to fourteen since he was twenty years old.

Researchers say that B is typical. He's married, like 77 percent of more than 5,000 self-admitted child sexual abusers questioned across forty-one states by the Abel and Harlow Child Molestation Prevention Study. And he's religious, like 93 percent of the abusers. The majority, like B, carry on normal adult relationships.

> *I had talked to women who were involved with organizations for abused women and they were ready to confront him at the pow wow and escort him off the grounds if he showed up. A clan mother was also involved. The grand chief told one of the councils to un-invite him. As for another pow wow, I shared at a women's gathering held here in Akwesasne and one of the women involved in its organization contacted the director for the annual event and made the decision to un-invite him as it was a family event. In all this he blames me for him being banned from two pow wows and getting fired. He doesn't seem to realize it's because of what he did, not that I told.*

In public he appeared gifted and good looking and those who didn't know him attributed positive traits.

Journey to the Edge of the Woods

I thought being persistent in opening discussion about the abuses would break years of silence.

"It's difficult," one woman explained. "I know someone who did all the right things—she went to the cops, she went to the hospital for testing. It's so much pressure on her. Court hearings have been postponed four times. She's a single mom. Then we learn that this same man did the same thing to three others and was never convicted."

As studies gathered in the UN's Permanent Forum on Indigenous Issues May 2013 report, Breaking the Silence Against Indigenous Girls, Adolescents and Young Women, they concluded that, "In all societies there are practices to keep, practices to change, and practices to reconsider."[3] Life for a traditional person continuing longhouse in a modern world means a way of living on the land and a way of giving thanks. There was no melting pot among the first nations, which is why absolute religious freedom could be established in North America. Being traditional also means a sense of purpose—belonging to a circle that brings friendship with others who are like-minded. Youth today seeing their peers being lost to outside influences, their future as a nation lost with them are cherishing the unity of a league brought forth by God's trusted design.

We are instructed, "For the grace of God has appeared that offers salvation to all people. It teaches us to say No to ungodliness and worldly passions, and to live self-controlled, upright and godly lives in this present age" (Titus 2:11–12). To do this, the letter to Titus instructs older women to show by example to younger women how to become mature, kind women. It instructs older men to be worthy of respect and live with dignity.

This tells us to turn the minds of others toward God, away from the shifting sands of the society that surrounds us, beyond the struggles faced by all women and "being confident of this, that he who began a good work in you will carry it on to completion until the day of Christ Jesus" (Phil 1:6).

---

3. UNICEF, "Breaking the Silence."

4

Community

I went to counseling after my arrest. I was very ashamed of all of it. Getting involved with him while I was still in my marriage, not being able to let it go to the point of getting in trouble legally as a result. It was almost a relief because it had begun to feel like an addiction. It wasn't only the relationship with him but my inability to form positive relationships in general. My counselor said the way we are raised can affect our future behavior but we can change it.

—Millie

Tamar was a princess, the daughter of King David and Maacah. She was an adolescent girl, not fully a woman yet, when she experienced how being beautiful could be a burden that brought trouble. Her half-brother Amnon was obsessed with her. He was David's eldest son and unused to anyone saying no to him. Conspiring a plan to get Tamar alone, Amnon pretended to be ill. He would not eat and told his father that he might be able to take food if Tamar cooked it and fed it to him. David sent for Tamar to take care of her brother.

Tamar went to Amnon's rooms, prepared the food and set it before him. Still pretending to be ill, Amnon ordered all the servants except Tamar to leave the room. He went into the bedroom alcove and insisted Tamar bring the food to him there. She followed and when she leaned forward with the food Amnon pulled her onto the bed and raped her.

Afterward he was disgusted at the sight of her. He shouted at her to get out of his room. Cast aside, a violated woman, Tamar wailed as she staggered through the corridors and found her mother. The women realized what had happened and Maacah pleaded with David to punish Amnon but David refused.

The brutality affected not just Tamar, but her mother, Amnon's mother, the sisters of Tamar and Amnon and every woman of the kingdom who heard of the incident. The men had failed to retain a structure of safety or bring justice.

Women bringing new life since the start of our lineage gained wisdom of the process of birth, mothering, being a grandmother, a sister, a daughter, and a friend who pass along the stories to other women. In Mohawk country this connects every female to the Haudenosaunee creation story of a pregnant woman, Iotsitsisen (Mature Flower) in Sky World. She was married to the Keeper of the Tree that gives off perpetual light to the world on this side of the sky. She wanted roots from the tree, which is an herb the tree of life offers. When she looked down a hole dug at the roots she saw a great darkness. As she leaned to look, she began falling through the hole and she grabbed seeds of tobacco, strawberries, and other plants.

The Sky Woman plunged toward earth when earth was covered by a deep ocean of water. To slow her fall a flock of geese stretched open their wings and guided her onto a turtle's back. A muskrat dove deep to the bottom of the water and brought up earth to place on the turtle. Sky Woman danced upon the soil, following the sun's light in a counterclockwise direction. As she danced and sang the songs she brought from Sky World, the earth

Community

expanded into a continent and she planted the seeds she held in her hand. The continent of North America came to be called Anonwarakowa, which means Turtle Island.

Sky Woman birthed her daughter Tekawerahkwa (Gusts of Wind), who learned to dance alongside her mother, counterclockwise as the women dance today in recognition of their responsibility to life continuing. These ceremonies follow the cycles of the living world, the plants, mother earth, the moon, and the stars, with the songs that were given long ago carried on today with water drums and rattles.

When Tekawerahkwa grew into a woman she became pregnant and birthed twins who together worked to make the creations around us. The story of the twins, Tawiskaron (Flint), the left-handed twin and Okwiraseh (Maple), the right-handed twin, showed the people there are balances in the creation. Birth and death, night and day, butterflies and biting insects all formed from the balances. When a trauma occurs to the land or to the water and people, the people ask what they can do to restore balance because from the first woman through the line of ancestors there is a heritage that sustained life and is intended to provide for their descendants.

When Sky Woman died, her body became part of earth and her head became the moon watching over earth, guiding the cycles of female reproduction. The moon is called Grandmother Moon, the oldest of the female cycles, providing a lunar calendar the faithkeepers rely on for remembering times to come together to renew thanks offerings. She looks after all the tides of earth, showing her face every twenty-eight days, reminding of the celebration of woman's role in the creation since the beginning of time.

Dependability abides in the cycles when women place jars of water under the sky to intermingle with the light of a full moon shining over the land. This brings women together, each coming from the problems of their lives, together uplifting their thoughts, replenishing the feminine, singing songs cherishing Creator's unfailing blessings over the past, present, and future.

Journey to the Edge of the Woods

In the acknowledgment of the moon is the remembering of Sky Woman nurturing the soil to provide haven for her daughter. The apostle Paul witnessed this inherent experience of women, nurturing not just a child, but gardens, projects, neighbors, ideas, and artwork. He noted how responsibility toward growth brought greater wisdoms in a woman's life.

Jesus demonstrated that life is not about our rights but about other's needs and to realize ourselves as one body needing every part's wellness. He tells of a magnificent desert land where a selection of trees would transform the landscape of the heart. The Cedar, used in cleansing, in the construction of Solomon's Temple and planted when a boy is born; the Pine, planted when a girl is born and used to carve the cherubim in the Hebrew's temple; Acacia that repels insects, used to construct the ark of the covenant and the altar; Myrtle, for the booths used during the feast of the tabernacles; Olive, that gave its branch for the dove as a symbol of peace and provides abundant oil; the Fir also used in Solomon's Temple and for musical instruments; Cypress, another evergreen that brings shade from the heat of the day and oils that promote circulation.

The combination of trees rising from a barren desert perpetuate God's promise to the oppressed to look beyond the earthly veil to his altar high above. Later, when Peacemaker came, he reinforced societies as part of the design of creation, their responsibility to combine gifts for a larger context, and for leaders to insure there will be a home for the sons and the births of daughters on land of their ancestors. Reminding that we carry our origins from the Sky World, the heaven pouring promise upon the sin-cursed earth, he was able to unite the warring factions by restoring sight of each person being made from the breath of Creator.

Elders trusted this design as a guide to help them guide others. Grandmothers lived intimately with the land that sustained their families. Reciting each species of tree to the children, calling the birds by name, the children around them listening were brought to understand the appreciation of all we've been given and how we are to live. The design of life belongs to God.

Community

A problem of the past still occurring today is that people believe Indian gatherings are to worship creation. There is limited understanding of the thanks given to Creator and thankfulness toward the creations acknowledging their work. For traditional people carrying on their heritage, this is a more direct communion with God than the splintered factions among church politics.

They listened to the land, the rhythms of the animals that live in balanced populations with each other, and the seasons of the plants that were used to strengthen health. Tobacco, a gift from the sky world brought by Sky Woman to help them speak to Creator, is left in return for taking a medicinal plant or thrown on fire as expression returning respect to sky, sun, and moon for crops and light that make life possible. At times the tobacco is placed in gratitude acknowledging *he'no*, the thunderers who are considered grandfathers, who with the west wind brings rain for harvest.

When the people assemble socially or politically the Words That Come Before All Else, the words of thanksgiving, are spoken before council opens and when it closes. Everything in creation is acknowledged and thanks are given that they continue especially in our days of toxins and over development pushing many species to the edge of extinction. Thanked too are the teachers sent to remind us how to live as people and thanks for the Great Mystery who dwells in the heavens and is the source of all life. The presence of the words of thanks in thought protect the mind. The apostles emphasized this need, saying, "Do not conform to the pattern of this world, but be transformed by the renewing of your mind. Then you will be able to test and approve what God's will is—his good, pleasing and perfect will" (Rom 12:2).

For our struggle is not against flesh and blood, but against the rulers, against the authorities, against the powers of this dark world and against the spiritual forces of evil in the heavenly realms (Eph 6:12).

Native Christian fellowships continue giving thanks for each intricately designed element sustaining life to the last generation. There are native songs drawing people to the Lord, ancient in the sound of hand drums and rattles as well as newer instruments.

There are church gatherings that display the flag of the Hiawatha Belt, the Two Row Wampum, traditional baskets, or have a Peacemaker wampum belt at their altar. Dr. McDonald's church in Ohio has a special belt that was woven by Ken Maracle and is called the Mingo-Methodist wampum belt. Ken, a faithkeeper of the Cayuga Nation of the Six Nations in Canada wove it to commemorate the gift of the church building from the Methodists to the Mingos.

"This is not syncretism, it is contextualization," Dr. McDonald says. "We are worshipping and praising the Lord in our way and still proclaiming Jesus as the Way, the Truth and the Life."

Jesus comes to brokenness within an individual and between cultures. When he had been on the cross for about six hours, mocked, beaten, and betrayed, Jesus said, "I thirst" (John 19:28). Here was Creator who had made the oceans and all the rivers, lakes, and rainfall thirsting for the water of life.

Let anyone who is thirsty, come to me and drink (John 7:37).

He thirsted for humanity to be restored to God.

For if, while we were God's enemies, we were reconciled to him through the death of his Son, how much more, having been reconciled, shall we be saved through his life! (Rom 5:10).

He thirsted for humanity to be filled with God's Spirit.

But the Advocate, the Holy Spirit, whom the Father will send in my name, will teach you all things and will remind you of everything I have said to you (John 14:26).

He thirsted for us to be quenched.

Never again will they hunger; never again will they thirst (Rev 7:16).

In the Mohawk language a word for water, *ohnekanos*, contains the spirit that brought us into life. When a birth is brought through water or a tree is renewed by rainfall, there is the physical need that is entwined with the spiritual relationship of the divine Creator touching new life.

Water unites life. Kinship ties to the places of water where washing was done, meeting there and talking with each other, swimming with children in the river that flows through their land. We are in a reciprocal relationship, giving thanks for water,

Community

affecting its very molecules with our songs of joy and words of compassion or negatively as science now finds, if our words are harsh and angry. A Mohawk woman doesn't cook for gatherings if her mind is in a broken or angry place because the influence on the world around her and what she serves others is strong.

It is a medicine. Used during birth, during burials, during naming ceremonies for babies, coming-of-age ceremonies, to cure illness, water is the elemental medicine that is with us through life. Native healers sing appreciation to the water in times someone needs to be cleansed from toxins or disease. Song from the birds all around the water in nature, the whales singing in the deep, the winds bringing music through the trees, reverberate into waters that return to us in the rainfall, all designed by God's plan.

Millie stands on the riverbanks where her heritage is rooted in the ancient land, sharing one source of life with the people. The St. Lawrence River surges past carrying stories of her grandparents, her relatives, their struggles, and their ability to survive. To her ears it contains the sound of heaven releasing replenishment. To her touch it cleanses and refreshes. Her sight takes in sunlit jewels shimmering on the currents and all the wildflowers, birds, and animals that come to drink. To her thirst, it is the only taste of quenching. And to her heart it brings a way to carry life to others.

For a moment the pain is alleviated as the river brings the fabric of her history to support her, the sound of heaven touching earth, a river's edge where elders and youth come together passing on skills and telling the stories that bring her home.

Pain so deep it cannot yet be spoken can be written on paper expressing the desperate cry of fears, and burned, its ashes cast into the river to carry away as the smoke rises as prayer to be heard in heaven. Letting the river wash away the dust and revive her, she gives thanks as the sun faithfully rises over its currents.

Because we again are experiencing pains, needing to hold a hand that won't let go as lawlessness convulses the land with violence and abuse, Jesus furnished us with insight: "All these are the beginning of birth pains. Because of the increase of wickedness, the love of most will grow cold. For then there will be great distress, unequaled from the beginning of the world until now—and never to be equaled again" (Matt 24:8, 12, 21).

Just as she reaches beyond the resisting wall, Millie's pains have exhausted her. She is swallowed in the pain, unable to see the new birth just ahead, at her last strength she cries.

As a pregnant woman about to give birth writhes and cries out in her pain, so were we in your presence, Lord (Isa 26:17).

She cries out for God's strength reflected in the river, emanating from the land, pouring from the sky. A much different perception of water and land came from across the ocean, valuing it for how it could be controlled for individual prosperity. The divergent thinking contained different attitudes toward women, impeding early relationship between the first people and the newcomers. Yet it would be these wounds to the ailing water, the violated women and wounded children that would begin to pull them together.

> *I grew up in a very dysfunctional family and was not able to trust that my mother could be there for me emotionally or physically. She said things to me that no sane parent should ever say to a child. I was told I had no looks, no personality. My counselor said that was why I tended not to trust people because I would end up disappointed. I'd experienced my mother's rages in her alcoholic state and that's how I tended to deal with things. Lash out first and think later if I felt I was being deliberately hurt. That's what I did with B. It took me awhile to trust him, I confided in him and he devastated me. I had such mixed feelings because I felt like I deserved his treatment of me.*

Like the birds catching Sky Woman and helping her softly land to stand upon the earth, the women came together to help each falling heart find solid ground. Sky Woman couldn't go back to where she was before she fell. She may have grieved for the loss of her world but she accepted her destiny to the new creation. She supplied plants that would stop the poisonous plants and illnesses that the darkness grew. She would take comfort in telling the twins about Sky World and nurturing life for her daughter. Embedded in the story is the concept of sacrifice for others.

Community

When women began to share their stories, words came out of the shadows like thunder, telling of addiction, suicides, abuse, and violence against children, women, and men. They spoke of daughters who had no father to swing them into the air or cover them in the night when they had a bad dream. They talked of women struggling alone to keep a home safe. Crying together for traumatized women, they wondered how to again raise sons to become respectful men who maintain reciprocity with women and children.

They took the harsh stories and rephrased their truth. Akwesasne women Beverly Cook, Jessica Danforth, and Katsi Cook created the Konon:kwe Council (Woman's Council), an instruction in the Great Law for them to keep a fire. Hawi Thomas joined with her expertise in law enforcement. Bear Clan Mother Louise McDonald and Randi Rourke Barreiro extended the circle, each bringing their strengths to the community. They became a safe place to turn where the mask of a smile was not necessary. The pain of the heart finds acceptance.

Millie attended a ten-week traditional healing program in which she did a ceremony to burn B's picture. As she watched, it took a long time disintegrating and seemed to represent her resistance to let go. She went through a ceremonial sweat that left her stronger but her anger felt clearer too. The tormenting thoughts of B with the young girls and the others who let him get away with it returned again and again, needing her to constantly renew her truths in ways heritage can help.

Not knowing how to trust even herself, Millie would have to lay a new foundation. She began in belief of bringing wrongs into the sunlight just as the women had always brought a leader's wrongs into the light of the day's responsibility.

> *I had known he was on probation years prior because I had wanted to invite him to speak at our gathering and he said he was on probation for a stupid offense and since smuggling was big at the time I had assumed it was that. Twice into our involvement I had asked him what his*

> *charges were but he wouldn't say. He'd just laugh it off or change the subject.*

In a conversation with the mother of the little girl he'd attempted to molest, Millie learned that it was a Saturday morning and B's wife went out to get groceries while her children from a previous marriage were still asleep. She got a frantic call from her daughter on her cell phone, crying, and saying that B had done something to her. The mother was so upset she told her to take her brother and lock themselves in the bathroom and she'd be right home. Brushing past B, she ran into the house and got her children out of the bathroom. She asked her daughter what happened. The little girl said that B woke her up and told her to get ready for the day. She had gone to the bedroom to get ready to take a bath and he went in there and asked her for a hug. She went to him and he put his arms around her and began kissing her neck, touching her and kissed her on the lips. She told him to stop but he said it was okay because he loved her but she told him if he didn't stop she was going to scream. He let her go and left the room and she called her mom. At 2:50 p.m. that afternoon he was charged with second degree sexual abuse and second degree endangering the welfare of a child, charges that don't merit being placed on the pedophile registry. He plead guilty and was given six years probation.

> *He said it was a mistake he made that ruined his life. I asked, what about the hurt it caused the girl and her family? But he never responded to that.*

In the US, a known 400,000 children are sexually abused every year with about 40 percent more cases remaining unreported, according to the National Indian Child Welfare Association and Casey Family Programs—an estimated one in every four girls and one in every seven boys.

Women of the fresh water rivers, women from wetlands and salt marshes, from brackish deep lakes and from the salt oceans began expressing the need for relationships that fence off harmful behaviors, a need referenced in Romans 6:6: "For we know that

Community

our old self was crucified with him so that the body of sin might be done away with."

Respect is one of the three rows in the Two Row Wampum that connect the two vessels. Respect—without which there is racism—not just for each other but one that encompasses our respect for God and for his care of all creation.

There is simple solution, native pastors say. If you see a need, don't wait for a church. Jesus builds relationship from the wounds. This has borne fruit among all genders and peoples, from Dr. McDonald's founding the Shiloh Community Center for Human Development in the 1980s to work done with migrant seasonal farm workers for La Raza Unida to community organization for the Ohio Hispanic Institute—all done through his Great Peace Native Fellowship, all involving giving a cup of cold water, such as is given at the edge of the woods, in the name of Jesus.

"I believe that the answer to helping these native women is to get out on the streets and do it!" he says. "It probably is not a job for many squeaky clean upper middle class non-native women but what they can do is support someone who will help them."

Dr. McDonald has walked the streets of Toronto ministering to homeless native people. Seeing that he was another native with a shared history on the land, one asked him to put down tobacco and pray for him.

"You just have to know where people are coming from before you can help them," he said. "Being one with them helps even more. When you do that and get other like-minded people to do the same, then you will see the women being helped and won to the Lord."

Dr. McDonald began Shiloh in an abandoned school building on a reserve that had the highest per capita rates of alcoholism in the state. They began with no funding, loading trucks in a warehouse to pay utilities, organizing people, and four years later were serving 8,000 people a year from five locations. His fellowship has now expanded to six countries on three continents serving native people in Canada, US, Ghana, Kenya, India and Pakistan. There is a Church of the Great Peace in all these locations, spreading by word of mouth and the Internet.

"The churches don't need more meetings and discussions about the Indians," he said. "They just need to begin to do something to fund some of the native-generated work." It's about the Two Row relationship.

The 1990 Native American Graves Protection and Repatriation Act (NAGPRA) requires federal agencies and institutions to return human remains and culturally identifiable items. Native people involved in repatriation have said it uses language deliberately "not created by Indians, but by those who possess our materials and have a vested interest in not returning it."

"The Society for American Archaeology would only support watered down legislation, whereby they would have exclusive control over the most relevant definitions, for example a difference between funerary v. unassociated, culturally affiliated or not, and this was very definitely a theme echoed by Iroquoianist' scholars," said Dr. Brian Broadrose, Seneca.

Dr. Broadrose spent five years collecting more than 800 documents and frequently finding unmarked boxes of bones in labs of schools in upstate New York as he worked on his 2014 dissertation, "The Haudenosaunee and the Trolls Under the Bridge: Digging Into the Culture of Iroquoianist Studies," for Binghamton University.

The scholars were dubbed the trolls, referring to mythological beings lurking under bridges who prevent native people and their history from connecting with Euro-Americans and their history. The dissertation talks about scholars persistently denying voice to the "Other" and preventing that bridge from bringing them together. The law as it is, he said, can be compared to finding the remains of a famous European like Shakespeare and not having to repatriate to Europeans.

"Because Shakespeare wore different clothing, spoke a different variant of English, and had different materials than Europeans use today, therefore he must not be European," he explained.

Community

"Many don't want anything to do with Indians as living breathing people. We're only a long ago history."

New York provides no protection for burials that are not marked by monuments in the Euro-American cemetery fashion.

"How is it that basic human rights that all other groups are afforded in the US, including control over ancestral remains and graves, can be compromised or negotiated?" Dr. Broadrose asked.

This is a hard truth to see beyond when non-native people approach indigenous people. The claim by one people of a right of dominance over another is being discussed at the UN Permanent Forum on Indigenous Issues where thousands of native people gather together every year. In 2010 Special Rapporteur Tonya Gonnella Frichner, a member of the Onondaga Nation and the US representative on the Forum, recommended a worldwide study to "provide an opportunity to understand that all the various struggles that indigenous peoples are engaged in are a manifestation of the same root cause."

Beyond the politics that wouldn't relent on extinguishing identity, it can be the churches who establish relationship of shared faith based on respect, friendship, and peace.

Jesus invites, "Whoever is thirsty, let him come; and whoever wishes, let him take the free gift of the water of life" (Rev 22:17). His words drew from the many provisions of water in the scriptures that speak God's promise of Christ to everyone in a dry and unjust land. When the people were thirsty crossing the desert, God instructed Moses, "Strike the rock, and water will come out of it for the people to drink" (Exod 17:6). "For they drank from the spiritual rock that accompanied them, and that rock was Christ" (1 Cor 10:4). Water trickled from the temple becoming a river in the vision of Ezekial (47:1–11). Water from Jerusalem was for the nations (Zech 14:8).

The Old Testament stories foreshadow the living water that Christ was to be after he ascended from the grave, to the Jew first and then to other nations. "The law is only a shadow of the good things that are coming—not the realities themselves" (Heb 10:1). These stories were retold at the Hebrew feast of tabernacles with the Celebration of Water Libation both in remembrance of the past and of God's promises for the future. A procession of priests would go out to gather willow branches to place along the altar, told of in the book of Leviticus. The people held four kinds of branches in their hands—myrtle, willow, palm, and citron to be blessed each day of the festival.

The high priest carried fragrant branches as he led the people in singing the Psalms. They proceeded from the temple through the water gate and walked to the pool of Siloam where the high priest filled a golden pitcher from the pool fed from the spring of Gihon. Returning to the temple, the priest carried the water, walking to the inner court to pour the water into the basin toward the west. As the water flowed before God, three trumpet blasts signaled the people to begin singing "Hallelujah! Praise, servants of Yahweh, praise the name of Yahweh. Blessed be the name of Yahweh, now and forever. From the rising of the sun to its setting, praised be the name of Yahweh!" (Ps 113). They waved their palm branches and sang "Hosanna! Save us, I pray, O Yahweh; Yahweh, I pray, send now prosperity" (Ps 118:25), and the other priests carried palm branches as they walked around the altar of sacrifice.

"Do not think that I have come to abolish the Law or the Prophets; I have not come to abolish them but to fulfill them," Jesus told his people (Matt 5:17). Every nation could relate to the representation of water being life. We can believe our need for this. The poor in spirit, thirsting for comfort can trust this and be quenched. Without that trust bringing comfort, there remains a traumatized distrustful community.

Speaking of the heart behind the fear in the community, a resident said, "I'm looking at our children as tomorrow's leaders. I want to know that our nation will still be here in fifty years and that we will be strong, healthy human beings. In light of all that we have endured, we're still here, battered and wounded but still here. We truly are a resilient people."

A land of fresh water lakes and rivers, the musical chirp of chickadees, quiet footprints of deer and foxes, and wildflowers providing sustenance for all life are inseparable from spiritual

Community

importance to the people. The creations are recited in the thanksgiving prayer with knowledge of how to use the roots and flowers of plants growing in meadows and forests, along water's edges and outside their doors, how to collect them and prepare them to prevent illness, or for sporting injuries, or to ease infections by using plants with antimicrobial properties. An abundance of aromatic bergamot in the woodland shade, stinging nettle or yarrow standing in sunny meadows, witch hazel, sumac berries and raspberry bushes providing teas and herbs bring gratitude to daily life. As new diseases arrived from across the ocean, there is thought that medicine may be provided in the new plants that also came and took root. The earth all around taught them that God's design was intentional and couldn't be changed without consequence, a thought that carried into the community of men, women, and children.

Woman became defined as someone independently successful. Dismissive of men, they no longer remembered the standard they were to carry or the importance of their influence as the female of God's image. Men began to fall into abuse, adultery, dismissive of commitment to women. Predatory sex addictions became labeled an illness offenders aren't responsible for, rather than as a spiritual evil in warfare against the victims. But no cure has been found. No amount of federal funding has defeated this.

Jesus has that power.

In Rahab's time there were two million slaves in the fortified city of Jericho, a condemned people holding no rank. A moment came when Rahab, thought to have been a prostitute, saw that God was moving and she had to make a choice. Trembling at her own personal risk, she saved the two Hebrew spies who had crossed the Jordan River where their people were camped out, waiting to reclaim their land. Rahab hid them under bundles of flax on her roof when soldiers came and demanded she bring them out. Because of her help the Hebrew people spared her when they attacked and seized the city. After her choice, she was full of certainty and pulled as many people as she could into the safety of her household.

Journey to the Edge of the Woods

In time she became the great-great grandmother of David, showing that bloodlines would not mean everything. It is the heart of faith that created the line of descendants leading to Jesus.

The troubles of the world will continue to increase. Our sons and daughters are preyed on every day living in a battle for their minds and bodies. Without the familiar and secure respect for mother and father that's embedded in attitude toward a child, the honor toward grandparents that carries respect for God, a structure is being lost.

Only one in ten sexually abused children will ever tell someone what happened to them. For these, the responses are mixed.

"I know three girls abused by B years ago were called liars," a friend of Millie's said. "One was sent away to foster care. One was told well you shouldn't be playing with boys. Once called a liar, that's it for them, they close up."

"All these victims need to have their fears addressed and removed which can only happen if they feel they have support. Public exposure and courage can do this but who will be the ones to start?" One community member said this as the night of the new moon arrived, marking the days to Midwinter Ceremony that draws the people's thoughts to children yet to be born.

The Great Law had brought them through struggles against unspeakable crimes of war, genocide, racism, and assimilation policies cascading into a generation left to struggle with generational trauma. Custom gave them a way to remember women's place of honor, enduring in the condolences mourned together at a woman's burial, reflecting Aiionwatha's compassion:

> The people, say: "Now we become reconciled as you start away. You were once a woman in the flower of life and the bloom is now withered away. You once held a sacred position as a mother of the nation. Now we release you for it is true that it is no longer possible for us to walk about together on the earth. Now, therefore, we lay it (the body) here. Here we lay it away. Now then we say to you, Persevere onward to the place where the Creator dwells in peace. Let not the things of the earth hinder you. Let nothing that transpired while you lived hinder

you. Looking after your family was a sacred duty and you were faithful. Now we release you for it is true that it is no longer possible for us to walk about together on the earth."

A generation growing up in a psychology to self-analyze began blaming their past for everything. They noted how their parents were not perfect and lost honor or gratitude for them. They lost compassion for the struggles of the elders and lost a sense of responsibility for the future.

> *That's the part that bothers me the most I think. I knew better and I don't know what I was thinking to go along with it. I knew deep down what kind of person he was coming onto me. As bad as things were discovering that his feelings were never real, I never imagined that he'd had such a past. Even when he had admitted to me that his charges were a sex offense, he claimed it was all a lie.*

There would be no undoing what the past had done. Like the river flooding, tossing about branches and leaves, spreading up over the land to cleanse and uncover roots, joy would return only in the new truth coming from within, a greater truth of God telling of who a woman is to him.

> *I've taken responsibility for my part in this. I made a mistake. He continues to blame everyone else and has never accepted accountability.*

A resident responded, "So what do our children think of all this, what are their impressions? Surely it can't be good or honorable. It is very frustrating to watch this and to ask: Why is this being allowed to happen? Of course Millie is angry, just as I am. Maybe someday our community can begin to heal."

Not stopped, acts of violation ripple through the entire community. When Tamar's brother, Absalom, learned about what happened to her he moved Tamar into his own house and tried to be a comfort to her. He went to David, demanding that Amnon marry his sister, but Amnon refused. David was upset but like many people, he did nothing when he learned of rape or incest. The abuser is protected by silence.

Absalom's anger raged and he planned revenge. Opportunity came two years later when he held a feast for David's sons. Absalom had Amnon stabbed then he escaped to Geshur. But the smoldering anger did not stop then. Years later Absalom led a revolt against David and took over the city of Jerusalem. Absalom took advice to rape all of David's women who were left behind so his father would know they were dishonored just as Tamar had been. But his reign in Jerusalem was short and he died a young man in a battle.

Absalom left his daughter, whom he named Tamar, fatherless.

> I didn't know until too late that I was involved with a child molester. My counselor thinks that discovering his past has triggered my own abuse which I never fully dealt with. I did go through a suicidal depression but that had started before I was involved with the guy . . . but what happened didn't help.

There are some 39 million adult survivors of child sexual abuse living in the United States today. We now understand this leaves a lifelong struggle with memories cast on the shores of every relationship and factors into our physical ability to maintain strong immune systems. It's the struggle between the positive and negatives continuing to demand choice, as recalled in the twins of dark and light, this time in the union of how a man and woman walk together, sensitive toward each other. But when Millie tried to save the "us" of relationship, B chose only to save himself.

Breaking the silence landed Millie in court and risked her career. But it also brought about a brave new communication between those who were harmed by an assault or knew about what was happening in their communities. Letters of support and explanation of dark secrets flew through the mail to the courtroom on her behalf from those who had once been afraid to speak.

"There will be a lot of people asking at some point, 'why didn't you guys do something sooner?'" said one elder. "I think about those who were hurt—do they think that no one cares?"

5

The Covenant of Forgiveness

Who lets mistakes in life define them? If we look at the founding of the Confederacy, Peacemaker came to restore. The idea of our Great Law is based on forgiveness and renewals. I have a lot to offer still. It doesn't make me someone to throw away. Handsome Lake (a Seneca leader who led the people to revive in the late 1800s) was once a terrible alcoholic yet Creator used him.

—B

The future of the Hebrew nation was in the hands of Moses. To accomplish this he is empowered by five life-giving women. At the time Moses was born the Pharaoh of Egypt was disturbed about the growing population of the Hebrews and ordered the midwives to drown all baby boys. But Shiprah and Puah couldn't bring themselves to do this and they saved the life of Moses when he was born. His mother Jochebed placed him in a papyrus basket to protect his life as she put it in the reeds of the River Nile. His older sister Miriam watched over him as the daughter of Pharaoh pulled the baby from the water and gave him a home. She then sent for a woman to nurse him and Jochebed had her son in her arms again.

Moses rose to become a tribal leader. As the people followed him out of the bondage of Egypt to cross a wilderness and find a promised land, Miriam rose too as a confident leader who also set an example for the people. Water was a theme in her life, from saving her brother from the waters, leading the women to dance and sing with tambourines after crossing the Red Sea, and the spring bursting abundant water when she died in the dry desert.

But Miriam was subject to her own thoughts. She and her brother Aaron began questioning the authority of their young brother Moses. As they crossed the weary desert Miriam began gossiping, disapproving of Moses' marriage to a Cushite woman, a foreigner. She stirred up the people's doubts.

God was listening. Her negative words lost the presence of his favor and she was struck by a skin disease. The book of Leviticus preserved the instructions to treat illness both medically and spiritually and Miriam knew she had to repent. She had to change. Her brother Aaron sought out Moses and asked him to pray to God for Miriam's life. She was healed.

In homeland communities there are stories that draw on these messages in ways each people can relate. Native pastors are offering spiritual training to develop warriors who understand the battles on their territories. They have unique insight into the many factors of family and resources that connect to a problem. They know who to intercede for and the circumstances to be shared. Cultural protocols bring recognizable ways for men to grieve and examples of healthy role models.

Battle fatigued, men have not healed when they push down their emotions to deal with life's every day challenges.

Three times as many men as women commit suicide. Male rape victims are in higher numbers under the age of twelve. Trapped in the cycle of having been devalued, the only power they may know is expressed as sexual abuse as anger festers at the world that did not protect them.

The Covenant of Forgiveness

Only 5,218 out of 16,109 offenders admitted they had a problem when questioned by the Abel and Harlow Child Molestation Prevention Study. The study found more than 40 percent of offenders molest before they reach fifteen, nearly all before the age of twenty. Often if the veil of secrecy is removed while an offender is still a youth, intervention is more effective, especially if they can see the reflection of an honorable man or woman in themselves.

As Peacemaker made his journey among the people he came upon a violent man who was cooking in a pot of water inside his cabin. When he didn't get an answer at the door, Peacemaker climbed onto the roof and looked down the chimney and saw the pot. When the man looked in his pot, he saw Peacemaker reflected in the water he thought he was seeing himself. When he thought such a handsome face was his own, he made the decision to stop killing other people. These two sides of human nature, the gifted and the hurtful, are in all of us.

When the man compared his inner self to the image Peacemaker brought, he realized his own degradation. He understood himself for what he was doing. Forgiveness of what others had also done came only after the realization of his own need to change. Renewing each other to these truths is a daily need every new day until Jesus returns and banishes the dark powers. But his offering that can transform how we are defined was needed only once, perfect and final.

Nor did he enter heaven to offer himself again and again, the way the high priest enters the Most Holy Place every year with blood that is not his own. Otherwise Christ would have had to suffer many times since the creation of the world. But he has appeared once for all at the culmination of the ages to do away with sin by the sacrifice of himself (Heb 9:25–26).

An emotional battleground fought for clarity in B's mind. Feeling guilt and wanting to be cleansed, both discouraged and hopeful, he stayed behind a wall of justification. Hearing so many different stories about Jesus and what he means to a culture clouded any relationship with this salvation before it reached him. When defenses fail and all he has tried has failed, the light can bring tears that help him see a new covering can be given to replace his shame.

Now Joshua was dressed in filthy clothes as he stood before the angel. The angel said to those who were standing before him, "Take off his filthy clothes."

Then he said to Joshua, "See, I have taken away your sin, and I will put fine garments on you" (Zech 3:3–4).

Peacemaker dismissed thought about whose side he had come to support and instead, invited all thought to be on his side. He became an earthly example of the commander of legions of angels, Jesus, cutting through the blame, commanding that we let go the bitterness and trust him to get us through the paths that he has already walked, conquered, and brought to victory.

It doesn't mean we'll understand the path. Millie would sit as Jonah beneath a tree, thinking how these people are useless, how they are failing justice. The apostle Paul modeled a response for us. Hammered by accusers among his own people, he intentionally addressed them as "brothers and fathers," beseeching them to hear the grace of God as people a part of himself. He didn't speak about the troubles he suffered, being left in a dark prison, being persecuted, or the plans to murder him. He held his focus on God's enduring desire for them (Acts 22).

We are told this story. Friends of a paraplegic lowered him through a roof to reach Jesus, expecting the man to be healed. "When Jesus saw their faith, he said, Friend, your sins are forgiven" (Luke 5:20). All healing begins with a step toward relationship with God in our need for forgiveness because it is then we begin to know who we are in our heritage with our Creator.

In churches there is sometimes a perception that everyone is thinking of how they appear to everyone else. When we are not considering how we appear to our Creator we can lose the opportunity for wounds to be understood and consoled. In traditional practices, such as a sweat lodge or walking into the woods for a plant someone needs, presence with God fills all the senses in a more direct communion. The edge of the woods condolence ceremony set an earthly symbol of the priority of being honest in our need, a turning of minds that can be together in unity.

The woods edge is a place where both tradition and western thought meet without one becoming the other, a blending where Jesus stands Lord of all nations. Relationship grows out of this ecotone, overlapping places that aren't native or non-native but the history and future of both. The protocol acknowledges that men have tears. The stories in the bible tell of prophets and kings weeping, fathers, sons, and brothers crying openly. When news of his son, Absalom's death reached David, "The king was shaken. He went up to the room over the gateway and wept. As he went, he said: 'O my son Absalom! My son, my son Absalom! If only I had died instead of you—O Absalom, my son, my son!'" (2 Sam 18:33). It had been his own lack of response to deal with the rape of Tamar that had set Absalom's course to destruction. Esau wept for his father's blessing. Jesus cried to God as his death approached. Peter wept bitterly at the sound of the rooster crowing, remembering his failure that had been predicted. Paul wept pleading with his people. The days of both Isaiah and Jeremiah were drenched with their tears.

Streams of tears flow from my eyes because my people are destroyed. My eyes will flow unceasingly, without relief (Lam 3:48–49).

Men cried even when others made fun of them. "My tears have been my food day and night, while people say to me all day long, 'Where is your God?'" (Ps 42:3). Sometimes they cried together. "So David and his men wept aloud until they had no strength left to weep" (1 Sam 30:4). They find strength in acknowledging their need for others. "My intercessor is my friend as my eyes pour out tears to God" (Job 16:20).

Akwesasne's domestic violence program combines the national Men for Change curriculum with traditional knowledge at the Iethinistenha Family Violence Shelter. The program uplifts men by reminding of heritage that carries reverence for women and wiping away their tears. Because of protocols embedded in the formation of their union as a powerful political force, they are allowed to cry here. They are shown the roots of their problem and how it has spread through the land. Guiding them to see the reflection of Peacemaker in themselves, all he endured walking among angry and frightened people, his discipline is passed on.

The program sees as Peacemaker saw, the tears behind the anger and tendency to justify behaviors. It gives a cultural map of pathways like the morning star that travels across the sky before the sun's promise of light.

Part of the past's thinking was in forgetting what is of value to our God. There is a deep sense of loss in men for the things left undone, a soul sense of a life that didn't serve God. Relinquished with prayer that his fear of being separated from God will overwhelm him, intercession needs to ask that offenders begin to have wisdom about consequences.

God is illuminated as a shepherd covering his sheep and asking our complete trust to the path the shepherd leads, believing he will lead us to springs of living water. If the shepherd is false, the sheep are vulnerable and left to thirst. "The thief comes only to steal and kill and destroy," Jesus warned. "I have come that they may have life, and have it to the full" (John 10:10).

Jesus told us the truth about fame, success, pleasure, and self-fulfillment leading to distorted relationship if these are the only goals. In his time alone in the wilderness when he was fasting and Satan presented images, sights, and sounds appealing to his ego, the book of Mark 4 records Jesus demonstrating how to walk through the barrage of temptations around us.

> "It is written: 'Man shall not live on bread alone, but on every word that comes from the mouth of God'" (v. 4).
>
> "It is also written: 'Do not put the Lord your God to the test'" (v. 7).
>
> "For it is written: 'Worship the Lord your God, and serve him only'" (v. 10).

He spoke the light in God's words and the enemy vanished. Angels came to minister to him. He wasn't left defenseless to debate or rationalize but had learned that knowledge of God is our

The Covenant of Forgiveness

impenetrable shelter. The thieves that come to rob our daughters of their covenant with God, offering false value to sexual intimacy, increasingly overshadow the knowledge of God's plan for men to be a covering for women against the assaults of Satan and for women to uphold the standard.

It is God's will that you should be sanctified: that you should avoid sexual immorality; that each of you should learn to control your own body in a way that is holy and honorable, not in passionate lust like the pagans, who do not know God; and that in this matter no one should wrong or take advantage of a brother or sister (1 Thess 4:3–6).

The Creator of all the stars and winds, every animal, plant and person, reduced himself to human form to share in our struggle. Even he, as a human, found no one would stand up for him in his hardest hour. In the garden of Gethsemane he wept unimaginable tears as he chose the pain ahead. His disciples slept as he called out to God. Peter would claim he'd never leave Jesus but at the moment of his testing, he failed God three times, denying even knowing Christ. Yet when Jesus rose from the grave and returned to the disciples, he opened his arms to Peter in a show of mercy that Peter was to anticipate seeing for every person willing to know Christ. It was only then, after experiencing his own limitations, that Peter could be commissioned to go to others.

The darkness inherent in our nature will not go away in a world with ever-falling standards of respect for the relationship between a man and woman. The disciple Peter repeatedly reminds us of all we've been given, an imperishable inheritance, salvation that even the angels long to look upon it. He sets our hope on the grace telling us, "As obedient children, do not conform to the evil desires you had when you lived in ignorance" (1 Pet 1:14). We are to choose justice, respect, and mercy because our hope has brought us to be children of a family. Again in verse 17 Peter instructs that we have one father, "Since you call on a Father who judges each person's work impartially, live out your time as foreigners here in reverent fear."

Journey to the Edge of the Woods

In Peacemaker's words is a method recognizable in all indigenous communities. The people were to act as members of a covenant family who have responsibility to consider what they are preserving for the next generations. When the men of the battle fatigued lands first gathered around Peacemaker and listened, the defenses against his message were well in place because of all the harm they had suffered. But they became the grandfathers, fathers, mothers, and grandmothers who taught it to the young.

One of the most intimate words in the Mohawk language is *rake'níha* ("my father"). The word should connote comfort, a dependable place of trust, a person who cares about our well being, and makes solutions possible. We want his blessing. It was his father who the prodigal son in Luke 15:11–32 ran to when he became destitute, coming home for his father to change his life, the example of support that guides beyond past missteps. A father's words spoken over the child remain for a lifetime.

"The Spirit you received does not make you slaves, so that you live in fear again; rather, the Spirit you received brought about your adoption to sonship. And by him we cry, 'Abba, Father'" (Rom 8:15).

God responds with assurances that quiet the fears. The message brought to Zacharias was "do not be afraid" (Luke 1:13), to Mary "do not be afraid" (Luke 1:30), to the shepherds "do not be afraid" (Luke 2:10), to James, John, and Peter "do not be afraid" (Luke 5:10), to the ruler of the synagogue "do not be afraid" (Luke 8:50), and to the apostle Paul "do not be afraid" (Acts 27:24).

Without elders to address emotions, acting as if their lives are without problem, men have lost children to abortion, lost their fatherhood, and don't speak of it. They press down the shame and confusion they carry. It's not supposed to matter, society tells them. Don't be weak.

An estimated 40 percent of children are being born in America to single mothers who often get driven below the poverty line trying to support a household alone—more than 24 million children without their fathers. Fatherless communities are a new condition on reservations left by centuries of breaking down the fabric of depending on each other. Men lost the training to protect and guide, do battle to guard against the enemy that now takes the shape of inner pain.

As the years forced the people onto tracks of reservations and the men could no longer provide fish and game for their hungry communities, the men fell into depression easily accessing alcohol. The women's hearts fell heavy and the young boys who would learn with their fathers, their uncles, and grandfathers were left without an ally. Back in the day men had a strong confidence in their surroundings. They lived oriented to how trees grow, how stars are fixed in heaven telling the time to go to hunt or to ceremony. Messengers knew the way home by the direction of star constellations, the Pleides (dancers), north pole (the star that never moves) Venus (she brings the day) and the Milky Way (the road of souls), a visible path to sky world. Their wish was to marry a good worker, a helper to provide shelter and sustenance, shelter his weaknesses and push his strengths. A man was in relationship with people of all ages as part of the group who provided safety for family and community because he enjoyed the path of good feeling. Disciplined since youth he had internalized ways to respond to challenges by growing up beside other men. A part of that training was the addressing the tears and pain that cause numbness, and the need for others to offer a cool drink of water. Giving the cool water is an act of acknowledging someone's pain or thirst.

The great adventures of succeeding crumbled under confusing messages about who they are in society today. Their chair in the home is empty. No one is there for the child who runs into the room. Diminished, the child holds it all inside and grows with the realization that family is not important to a dad.

Warriors lost in the battle of these forces become unable to foster connection, leaving others to shoulder the problems, locally or nationally, but impersonally as strangers to a child or mother. At creation, whether the Christian telling in the book of Genesis or the native way of telling the story, there was a universal instruction given to human beings. Give thanks and be responsible for the creation around you.

Breakdown with a divorce every fifteen seconds across the continent has been tearing apart the threads of an entire nation. This is irreplaceable. We need relationship with men in that circle around us. We need them to bring in the heavy logs and build a fire and have the place of value as the one near to us.

A result of relationship sin is in pushing blame onto someone else. Eve says the serpent made her eat of the forbidden fruit. It's his fault. The man Adam says to God "you put her here." He was saying that it was the fault of his circumstances, and his circumstances were God's responsibility.

But God had warned them the greater shelter of life is in peace with God. When a man picks up the responsibility again he is lifted up and becomes a part of the health of all life around him. In B's generation all older men were called uncles. Men who were elders were all called his grandfathers. Dances of festivals saw fathers in the circle with daughters, grandmothers with the sons in one accord giving thanks.

A father gives his daughter's hand into the hand of the man he trusts will care for her, taking him in as a son, reminding of her value, that he is to be trustworthy. Carried in this is the yearning and instinctive expectation to be together eternally because Creator's glory prevails.

The hours lived of childhood that begin with elders as trusted counselors, hearing the people give thanks as part of everyday life, and stand against offenses teaches girls to push upward against the tide of the world that crushes. The roles of female and male faithkeepers, aunties, clan mothers, and the assurances of a father or uncle as she grows, root a young girl to become a respected grandmother of dignity.

But encourage one another daily, as long as it is called "Today," so that none of you may be hardened by sin's deceitfulness (Heb 3:13).

The importance of daily encouragement reminds a boy that every time he acts on a wrong thought he is supporting the work of the destroyer. Another man who will go to him and speak privately if he is falling off the path is instructed, "If your brother or sister

The Covenant of Forgiveness

sins, go and point out their fault, just between the two of you. If they listen to you, you have won them over" (Matt 18:15). Paul, in advising how to take care of each other, said to do this in the spirit of meekness overtaking him with God's truths about the importance of who they are to be. A man openly admitting his mistakes brings courage to the others to do the same. The river flows in the land for the offender too. He can come and remember heritage from God. He can look at his memories and write the name of everyone he has harmed and the river will carry it too and the smoke rise in prayer to heaven.

The relationship of male and female is designed to reflect God's redeeming glory.

In the Lord, however, woman is not independent of man, nor is man independent of woman. For as woman came from man, so also man is born of woman. But everything comes from God (1 Cor 11:11–12).

Women set a tone and the men in a community rely on them to hold positions in esteem. *Royaneh*, women of good mind, will prepare food for the leaders when they meet together, an expression of respect for those around her making decisions.

As confusion deteriorates this relationship, more and more women began filling the prisons. Many are mothers leaving young children with others. Youth are committing violence against elders, mothers against their own children or husbands. As bonds with mothers, sisters, and daughters break down, abuse without conscience and without remorse is spreading. Where once children played freely and hugged with affection, they're told now to keep distance, no one has the right to touch them and they have no right to touch anyone.

> Millie said, *I was told that B had witnessed his mother taking money from men in exchange for sex. I learned more about the kind of mother he was raised by and found there were former neighbors who told horror stories about how verbally and physically abusive she was to the youth. She's cursed at them and snapped ears with her fingers.*

Abused as a child, how does a boy grow up respecting women when survival depended on holding down his susceptibility to wounds. How can he regain the integral bond of what has never developed in him?

> B went on to say, *"I don't know why it keeps coming up. It's hurtful to my family. It's a tough thing all around. It's hurt me at all levels. I don't think it's fair that it's still a factor. For centuries there's nothing on the topic, now this sudden overkill. We can go to the other extreme."*

A child in pain grieves openly. They haven't yet put on layers of pretense or been taught it is forbidden to show emotion. This openness draws our immediate response to comfort them. If not comforted and unable to mourn, he'll be framed in denial determined to have his own outcome, the way B responded. Instead of dealing with his own problems, he turns to an involvement with Millie or hunts a young girl.

The pain becomes more distant from reach. We don't see it as easily. We cannot reason with abusers because the way the world was during the time of battling before a Great Way was all that was known about how to respond in that world.

All of creation and the sky world is there to aide our physical and spiritual strength. Our crying can end because God cried for us. Sending us teachers, prophets, and his own son, the Lord continually reminds us that he hears our heart cry, "Create in me a pure heart, O God, and renew a steadfast spirit within me" (Ps 51:10). Basing all of life on what Jesus can do, "leading us not into temptation" we can respond together with a new heart to a society that wars against our efforts. "Hallowed be thy name." It is about who we believe.

Lord, the God of heaven, the great and awesome God, who keeps his covenant of love with those who love him and keep his commandments, let your ear be attentive and your eyes open to hear the prayer your servant is praying before you day and night for your servants, the people of Israel (Neh 1:5–6).

In the fifth century the biblical leader Nehemiah was purifying the remnant of his nation. In his response to security threats he says "we made our prayer unto our God, and set a watch" (Neh 4:9). We are to be watchful for the enemy in the land, the temptations or the messages that will lead away our children. This applies to being sure the sons and daughters are not left without instruction. They are made aware of the expectations of God for them to continue the knowledge for others and of the dangers of false shepherds.

When Peacemaker planted the peace tree, he spoke of an eagle who can see far distances and warn people of dangers coming. Today the eagle warns of long-term effects of trauma if we do not address the problem with condolences and if we don't stand on God's instructions. To maintain awareness of our need, the Thanksgiving Address was given to remind us of how dependant we are on respecting life and each other.

The cold, gray winters that cover Haudenosaunee land instill thankfulness for the covenant of spring when the fruits will again produce nourishment and the sun warm us. Together both the women and men of each clan prepare for festivals at each nation's longhouse. It is a tangible communion, with the scent of the fresh pine of the longhouse, the taste of healthy foods, the warmth of fire, sight of neighbors sharing the bounty, and the sound of songs sung to God.

As the women bring the balance of water, the flames from Brother Sun that are the male's provision of warmth and light foster growth. Giving thanks especially in times that are bad is what keeps the seven layers of resistance against unthinking responses. This came from God who spoke through the Hebrew people "give thanks in all circumstances; for this is God's will for you in Christ Jesus" (1 Thess 5:18).

Reaffirming the power of life to renew and thaw our hardened hearts, skilled like warriors carrying protections, the men were given the task of presiding over the Ohenton Karihwatehkwen, the Thanksgiving Address. The thanks offerings acknowledge the Creator's presence in all the elements of life. The words bring kinship, enforcing knowledge of where a person fits into the larger clan, their nation, the Confederacy, rooted together on the earth they live upon, beneath the heaven above. There is a thanksgiving in every language around the world in shared need to express gratitude. It is a harmony of the one heart of all nations.

We are in this battle for life. Temptation is never done with us. The words of Jesus tell us "For it is from within, out of a person's heart, that evil thoughts come—sexual immorality, theft, murder, adultery, greed, malice, deceit, lewdness, envy, slander, arrogance and folly" (Mark 7:21–22).

Peacemaker told the people their protocols are to remain with the people through each generation because they would prepare the young for challenges to come. If the thanksgivings are forgotten, the fighting and fear could return. At the center of that change was Tadodaho. He was the cruelest among the people, living in Onondaga land and practicing witchcraft and violence. It was Tadodaho who was responsible for the murders of Aiionwatha's daughters. It took Aiionwatha's forgiveness and the collective efforts of the people to come to Tadodaho and clear the twisted thoughts from his mind. They did this with ancient songs of life and by telling him they saw him able to fill an honored position. He became the League's first spiritual and political leader, a position that continues today. His past behaviors were not thrown back at him as he took on the new role. The people wanted healing. They wanted hope of the Comforter, Councilor, our Teacher the Holy Spirit that does not come to accuse but to reconcile us to God. It is the work of the enemy, the accuser, who continues reminding of past failures to keep people divided after a person had transformed through honesty.

> *I feel like that Pig Pen character from Charlie Brown. Everywhere he goes he carries a cloud of dust surrounding him. It seems I often burn a lot of bridges.*

Millie's past hung over her. B would not acknowledge the pain he caused. She could find no justice that would free her. The deep tearing in her soul would not be silent. But who could look at her and understand this? Paul, the apostle, spoke of a thorn in his flesh, a messenger from Satan that tormented him. "Three times I

The Covenant of Forgiveness

pleaded with the Lord to take it away from me. But he said to me, 'My grace is sufficient for you, for my power is made perfect in weakness'" (2 Cor 12:8–9).

Paul was burdened under crippling regrets of his past harming believers before he came to faith. It took time for others to accept he had changed. Pain of regret can move a person forward but often, even within a church, becoming busy with programs and activities to fill the spaces that being consoled should bring. Mistakenly told that anger, grief, and fear are expected to vanish when we come to the Lord, the feelings are compartmentalized and silenced so we can appear to have a healthy spiritual life. The wound remains more painful than when the wrong thing happened.

Another generation would tell men they were to be about "feelings" and talking about feelings, but their male nature wanted the action of accomplishing solutions. A renewed adventure would come, one of opening new territory with other men in restitution of identity. The men are beginning to examine their changing roles and talk openly about enclosed reserves controlled by the government, depressed expectations that have taken away their abilities to provide and mentor, the loss of fathers and grandfathers to the whole community that left boys being socialized by their peers.

The power of the good mind buried weapons of war a thousand years ago. Choosing this brought thinking collectively and considering everyone's points of view. Laboring the ground for food, the forests for meat, the rivers for fish, were benefits that were shared. No one went hungry. This worth came from responsibility to family, clan, nation, confederacy, and creation because there was a concept of a Great Mystery that had designed a plan. Each of the nations on the continent realized this higher power that guided life. This foundation in their origins is what they bring to the global body of the people choosing the Lord.

Reconciling relationship between the people began with restoring minds to the greater plan of Creator. But who would tell B of what he already knows? Who would help him be accountable and remind him how much it matters?

Journey to the Edge of the Woods

When the world was young, the men were given the game of lacrosse out of the struggle between Flint and Maple. The twin brothers agreed to have a contest playing lacrosse to determine who would have control but although they played from sunrise to sunset, neither won. After competing at other games they agreed Maple would hold sway over the daylight hours. Flint was to hold the balances of darkness. This is why meetings to make decisions are made only in daylight hours when the good-minded twin rules.

When the good-minded twin made *onkwehonwe* ("real human beings") he gave them the game of lacrosse so they would remember the dual influences over their minds. It is considered a favorite game of Creator who enjoys the high spirit of people giving their best enthusiastically. The game was played at the renewals of a new year to give thanks to the Creator and played to lift spirits when someone was ailing.

When the men are playing they are remembering the creation story, remembering to be thankful for all that they have been given, and their responsibilities on behalf of all life. Those watching remember too that the two brothers—the two balances—are still in a contest for control. The opposing forces mean that choices must be made to keep balance in the world. The cheering audience wants teams to win, putting aside individual differences. The importance of team success over individual goals is stressed to each of the fifty leaders of the Confederacy who Peacemaker instructed:

> "In all of your deliberations in the Confederate Council, in your efforts at law making, in all your official acts, self interest shall be cast into oblivion. Look and listen for the welfare of the whole people and have always in view not only the present but also the coming generations, even those whose faces are yet beneath the surface of the ground—the unborn of the future Nation."

To strengthen this understanding, the Peacemaker took five arrows and bound them together, each arrow representing one of the original nations. He did this to illustrate that unified as one body with one mind they could not be broken in their deliberations for future generations.

The Covenant of Forgiveness

Learning forgiveness from elders, how they present with diplomacy to bring minds together on what we all agree is important for our children, we witness how the elders stand, informing of past injustices but facing forward to lead a way out to know "God cares," awakening the heart's deepest longing.

Before calling the men to stand in a circle, the act of putting down weapons was a realization of forgiveness before he told them the governance is placed in their hands and they must defend this peace. The *roiane* are described as trees standing together in a circle around the people, their roots deeply entwined, their arms joined so that if anything were to fall on them, it would not separate their unity in protecting the people. To symbolize this union at each condolence of a new leader filling the position, a feast is held served from one bowl, signifying they are to share the land making sure that all have enough. No sharp utensils are used to signify no use of sharp divisive words. They are not to let their people go hungry but always put the people's needs before their own.

They recite Peacemaker's message:

"Hearken, that peace may continue unto future days!

Always listen to the words of the Great Creator, for he has spoken.

United people, let not evil find lodging in your minds.

For the Great Creator has spoken and the cause of Peace shall not become old

The cause of peace shall not die if you remember the Great Creator."[1]

They mentor youth for the future, realizing the message Peacemaker gave them warned of a day to come when they would nearly lose their grip on their knowledge of how to be unified. At that time many children would be born into the world. Among them would be those who understand how burdened the people are and would bring strength to protect their people.

1. Murphy, "Constitution."

Our preparedness in responding to the young coming up behind us relies on the interactions of the men and women around us sending messages into the future. As spiritual warfare strengthens attacks on the minds of the young, there are still those among us who are the salt of the earth, preserving the meat of the word for the next generations. The peoples across continents are beginning to share this knowledge. Native women such as Audrey Shenendoah, Eel Clan Mother of the Onondaga Nation, are more frequently speaking with women of other cultures. "We need to recognize the time our children are passing into another age," she says. "We need to recognize the stresses upon them. We have a big job as women to always remember our future generations depend on what we pass on. All of women should feel this honor."

Reflective time in solitude directly with God, listening, aware, enables a man to "Put off your old self . . . and put on the new self, created to be like God in true righteousness and holiness" (Eph 4:22–24). In it is a new song, "I delight greatly in the Lord; my soul rejoices in my God. For he has clothed me with garments of salvation and arrayed me in a robe of his righteousness, as a bridegroom adorns his head like a priest, and as a bride adorns herself with her jewels (Isa 61:10).

According to the Center for Disease Control and Prevention, almost 40 percent of native women and nearly 20 percent of native men experienced violence at the hands of their partners. How many people have witnessed an abuse and turned the other way. How many fathers and mothers, sisters and brothers, grieve helplessly not finding justice.

Be cheered, we can say. Jesus is calling your name.

6

The Longhouse

There was no one to help me. There was no one to stop him. The mother that should've helped me was often drunk out of her skull either having a drinking party in the house or off at a bar somewhere. Oftentimes when she was out she would return home and wake up everyone in the house with her ranting and raving and we would be in bed listening to the shattering of glass, pots and pans, food being thrown all over the kitchen. Once, we came downstairs to find the TV screen smashed because she had smacked a cast iron frying pan against it shattering the screen. Sometimes we'd walk into the kitchen to find food splattered all over, or the refrigerator tipped over and its contents spewed all over the floor.

—Millie

There was a prophetess named Anna who was among the first to recognize the face of God. She had been married as a young woman for seven years before her husband died. For the rest of her life, until she was eighty-four, she was a widow continually going to the temple to give thanks to God and fasted and prayed night and day (Luke 2:36–38). All those years as she grew old she waited for the prophecy of the Holy One who was to come and redeem her people. The day came that Mary and Joseph brought their newborn son Jesus to the temple to offer the custom of a purification sacrifice. Luke's Gospel describes Anna approaching them and recognizing what others didn't see. She begins to tell everyone, speaking of the hope that she has waited to see born in a child.

In a culture that increasingly ignores God's sovereignty, consequences are revealed in the plight of women and children around the earth, often in our own homes. Domestic violence is increasing. Child abuse is in every community. Human trafficking of women and children is expanding.

Laws stiffened with the 1990 Indian Child Protection and Family Violence Prevention Act and Congress began requiring mandatory reporting of suspected child abuse, ensuring training for investigation and programs for communities to protect children. In 1992 the U.S. Department of Justice Criminal Division expanded the Child Exploitation and Obscenity Section to bring aggressive prosecution of child sexual abuse.

Women of faith from every heritage have pushed for the laws. Knowing too that Christ did not come as a ruler of earthly government, but still today comes softly to the tears of the broken hearted, they seek beyond the consequence of laws to seeing women as Christ sees us.

But he, because he continues forever, has an unchangeable priesthood. Therefore he is also able to save to the uttermost those who come to God through him, since he always lives to make intercession for them (Heb 7:24–25).

In Akwesasne, drones fly high over the border that cuts through their community. The customs crossing has one of the most sophisticated surveillance in the country with listening devices, chemical detectors, x-ray equipment, and weighing vehicles. Jurisdiction over the 22,000 acres has been assumed by eight governmental entities.

The Longhouse

If Peacemaker returned to check on how the people are doing, he'd see there are those who have reached down and pulled out some of the weapons buried beneath the tree of peace. Some would argue these weapons are needed.

"There is no 'we' in the US Constitution," said a Mohawk man the people call Popeye. Popeye looks out across the highways, the houses in neighboring towns, businesses and schools, and he sees Indian land. He says the US Constitution is the written side of the Two Row Wampum.

"Everything embodied in it is the will of the people. In order to occupy Indian lands the Constitution, in Article 1, Section 2, Clause 3, excludes Indians from their laws of taxes," he says.

When he and his family were being evicted from a nearby town and he asked the police why they were doing this, the sergeant answered, "to protect the race." Chilled by the words, Popeye said, "I have children here. I don't want trouble. I got out my status card so there's no confusion. Here's my certificate of being Indian. It's not a retail card just to let me buy tax-free. It's a card that shows it's me the Constitution refers to, an Indian excluded from their law."

Popeye describes God coming to Moses on a mountain to give the instruction to the people not to pervert the words of the righteous. The verse (Deut 16:19) is listed in Common Legal Principles, published in 1929 by Massachusetts Judge Francis W. Marshall, stating canons adopted by the American Bar Association in 1924. Among them is a list of ancient precedents.

And I charged your judges at that time, "Hear the disputes between your people and judge fairly, whether the case is between two Israelites or between an Israelite and a foreigner residing among you. Do not show partiality in judging; hear both small and great alike. Do not be afraid of anyone, for judgment belongs to God" (Deut 1:16–17).

"All these people, all these politicians and DA's and sheriffs, state police and judges, have sworn to uphold their laws," Popeye said. "They swore on the bible when they took that oath of office. That'd be a good place to start wouldn't it."

Journey to the Edge of the Woods

In 2014, Gov. Andrew M. Cuomo reached a preliminary agreement with the St. Regis Mohawk Tribe (SRMT), St. Lawrence County, and the New York Power Authority in response to a Mohawk land claim first filed in federal court in 1989. The memorandum of understanding guarantees the Mohawk would be able to buy about 5,000 acres from willing sellers bordering their land and add the parcels to the reserve, waive tuition fees to state universities, and receive lowered electricity rates. The memorandum was also being negotiated with Franklin County where an additional 7,700 acres could become part of the reservation. The state would pay the counties any loss of property taxes.

The agreement was the first progress with six nations land claims since the 2005 US Supreme Court decision City of Sherrill v. Oneida Indian Nation dismissed an Oneida Nation suit because the nation had waited too long to file and it would disrupt those now living there.

The first footnote in the Oneida's Sherill case notes the Doctrine of Discovery. The Doctrine is a series of Vatican documents and Papal Bulls originating in the fifteenth and sixteenth centuries justifying colonial powers taking away lands from indigenous nations. Christian explorers were told lands they discovered were there for their Christian monarchs to exploit, regardless of the occupants, based on the racial superiority of European Christian people. It was used to dispossess indigenous peoples of their most basic rights, including using government to sterilize un-consenting American Indian women.

In 1985, the Supreme Court ruled New York treaties taking Oneida lands had not been authorized by the federal government. The US Supreme Court stated:

> "Despite Congress' clear policy that no person or entity should purchase Indian land without the acquiescence of the federal government, in 1795 the State of New York began negotiations to buy the remainder of the Oneidas' land. When this came to the attention of Secretary of War Pickering, he warned Gov. Clinton and later Gov. Jay, that New York was required by the Non-intercourse

The Longhouse

Act to request federal commissioners to supervise any land transaction with the Oneidas. The State ignored these warnings, and in the summer of 1795 entered into an agreement with the Oneidas whereby they conveyed virtually all of their remaining land to the State for annual cash payments. It is this transaction that is the basis of the Oneidas' complaint in this case."[1]

The landmark ruling entitled all Oneida to a settlement on the 250,000-acres in central state that had been given in the Canandaigua Treaty of 1794. But in Sherrill v. Oneida the Supreme Court determined the Oneida had to pay taxes on land reclaimed through purchase despite the former court ruling that they held title.

The case also lost the Cayuga Nation a settled land claim. In 2000 a jury determined the state had illegally taken the 64,015 acres on the north side of Cayuga Lake in 1795 and 1807. US District Court Judge Neal McCurn ruled that the state pay land claim damages totaling $247.9 million. Governor George Pataki announced a memorandum of understanding in 2004 with the Cayuga Nation to give the $247.9 million over fourteen years for the people to establish up to 10,000 acres of sovereign land.

In June 2005, the US 2nd Circuit Court of Appeals cited the Sherrill decision and reversed Judge McCurn's decision. Governor Pataki broke off the settlement with the Mohawk that had guaranteed the people $100 million and ability to add 13,400 acres contiguous to the reservation. The original claim was filed by all three Akwesasne councils—the SRMT that represents the New York side of the community, the Mohawk Nation Council (MCA) representing on the Canadian side, and the traditional Mohawk Nation Council of Chiefs (MNCC) that serves all Mohawk. Based on the 1790 Non-Intercourse Act that forbids purchasing Indian lands without the approval of the federal government, it argues that the state sold their land to settlers through the nineteenth century.

The original claim sought compensation for the lost lands, expanding jurisdictional powers, protecting tax-free status, and

1. U.S. Supreme Court, "County of Oneida."

eliminating problems of the international border that bridges New York and Canada through their community. An appraisal in 1988 estimated the value of the lands at more than $400 million from which Mohawk could seek more than $69 million in annual rental fees.

At a community meeting held in summer 2014 Doug George-Kanentiio, member of the original negotiating team in the 1980s, made a plea for the tribal council to remember that there's a process of consensus for the people to accept this and with only the tribal council needed to bind the community, this completely rejects all that they had done.

"A cardinal rule that guided us is that land be returned unconditionally," he said. "At no point did Mohawk people agree to cede even an inch of our land, which should have been a lead in this negotiation."[2]

The other two councils are not included in the memorandum. The traditional council stated, "The Tribal Council does not speak for the Mohawk Nation. We would like to take this time to point out that the MOU was never made available for review by the Nation and was never presented at any session of the Mohawk Nation Council of Chiefs, nor has the Mohawk Nation leadership agreed in council to support any version of the MOU. Our political system is based upon consensus and no consensus decision has been made to support the MOU." SRMT Chief Beverly Cook said that the agreement would bring land back to the people and going further through the courts only loses them more each time. "We addressed their needs and the self-interest to which all businesses and homeowners respond: lower taxes, a tidy profit from land sales, increased economic opportunities and mutual respect," Doug said. "We used old style Mohawk traditional values such as cooperation, alliances, clarity as our principle guidelines under the Great Law."

The Two Row Wampum extended from the Great Law of Peace and abided between all the nations of North America long before the Dutch arrived. It is a statement that we share the earth

---

2. Akwesanse Community Meeting, June 11, 2014.

The Longhouse

as distinct and equal peoples. If we see the two separate vessels as unique and the water we are all drawn to as the living waters of Christ, the message is for each to be responsible for their own earthly governance and policies and act in respect to each other.

Under the Great Law the village of houses is a congregation endeavoring to bring each person into the tradition of giving thanks. In the center of the village is the longhouse, the place to consecrate self and affirm that Creator's instructions bring blessing. It's a place to give expressions of gratitude. Afterward the people gather to fellowship and share food that celebrates the Creator's faithful provision.

The collective expressions affirm, "We are the Haudenosaunee people." Each nation of the world has their unique expression of this tradition. When they visit each other's territories, they come in respect for how giving thanks is done in each place. The people who come out of this gathering to partner with environmentalists, towns, and educators to restore health to our suffering waters are those who come out of these buildings where tradition affirms their relationship with God. They are the people coming from giving thanks for all of creation, for each other, and for God. They are those who receive the condolence of the Edge of the Woods to transform others before meetings convene.

When the newcomers came to Haudenosaunee lands, the protocol of the woods edge was extended to them, the thanksgivings spoken during each treaty-making, reflected in sharing knowledge of planting and harvesting in a new environment, pathways of travel along rivers, and in the respect for religious freedoms and the sharing of the Great Peace that became the blueprint of America's Constitution.

All of northeastern New York was called *Kanien'keh*, "land of the flint," Mohawk Nation territory. The Dutch came, then the French, and then the English. The English fought with the Dutch, and later the French fought with the English and after that the English fought with the Colonies, and in most cases the Indians were drawn in to the wars. Then the story was told of April 27, 1797 when the state gained 6 million acres of the Adirondack

Journey to the Edge of the Woods

Mountains through a treaty that would have been null and void if they had dealt with the leaders of the Haudenosaunee.

The treaty said

> " . . . it is thereupon finally agreed and done, between the said agents, and the said deputies, as follows, that is to say: the said agents do agree to pay to the said deputies, the sum of one thousand dollars, for the use of the said nation, to be by the said deputies paid over to, and distributed among, the persons and families of the said nation, according to their usages."[3]

The Mohawk "deputy" who signed the treaty, Joseph Brant, sold his people's country without their knowledge or consent. A military leader who fought for the British from 1775 to 1797, he was a Mohawk soldier of Canada not following the constitution of the Haudenosaunee that requires the meeting of all leaders of the six nation league for any decision regarding land.

"Inalienable means the land is inseparable from us," Popeye says. "Yet everyone draws a check and benefits from the wealth of Indian resources. It takes and takes and it kills and it doesn't see it's killing all our children."

All the protections of the Bible are shrunk down to nothing, he said. "Everybody in the world is trying to get us to say we're not Indians."

This day is holy to our Lord. Do not grieve, for the joy of the Lord is your strength (Neh 8:10).

The Bible tells us we are to have joy at the same time telling us troubles in the world will worsen. It is his joy in redeeming us that brings us strength. But like Popeye many native people of the world see a system carrying the bible either to ignore it or to use it to justify injustice. Lawlessness will spread until the day Jesus returns. There will be those under relentless oppressions and a continuing need to encourage and comfort. Even those who bring the message of redemption are limited in their humanness.

---

3. Kappler, ed., "Treaty with the Mohawk, 1797."

The Longhouse

Scripture reminds how womanhood brings about a legacy of consoling those in exile when attention is drawn away from messengers who may falter and kept on the risen Lord. "Shake yourself from the dust and arise; be seated, O Jerusalem; loose the bonds from your neck, O captive daughter of Zion" (Isa 52:2). God's intent is for the balm to go to the exiled as the angel proclaimed to the women at the tomb, "Go quickly and tell his disciples that he has risen from the dead" (Matt 28:7). Urgently, tell the news to those who yearn in hope, Jesus rose, he is alive, and he has brought victory over every darkness.

Let the redeemed of the Lord say so, whom he has redeemed from trouble (Ps 107:2).

Thirsting for redemption brought about a gathering place of women of all nations where prayer propelled an expanding circle, increasing the guidance to others and safety again began to encircle the community. Each doing their part, each is fragrant with the gift of gathering at the woods edge.

The Mohawk community's Konon:kwe Council meets with women from each of the Confederacy's six nations to bring together the Haudenosaunee Coalition for Women's Empowerment. In turn, HCWE joins with the National Indigenous Women's Resource Center to collaborate healing their victims of assault as a part of honoring Mother Earth.

They join with the Maori of New Zealand, Wara Wara of Australia, the peoples of the Lakota, Tibetan, and Hawai'i nations of people coming out of the shadows to speak of disruptions to womanhood. Their voices came to the UN where a Commission on the Status of Women had been created in 1946 to begin documenting the lives of women around the world in a need for education and employment. By spring 2013 the Commission's theme was "Elimination and prevention of all forms of violence against women and girls." Testimonies brought to light how girls had to walk long distances to find clean water in communities where water was contaminated or had dried up. This left them vulnerable, especially in countries in Latin America where an estimated 36 percent of the indigenous population younger than 18 had little access to safe water.

It was found that most of the world's 15.5 million children in labor for domestic work were young girls, isolated with a lack of social support. Children were 27 percent of the victims of human trafficking. More than 67 million women, half in Asia and many in Africa, were given into marriage when they were young teenagers, leaving them without option and unequipped to protect themselves from the epidemic of HIV/AIDS.[4]

At the time the UN's Declaration on the Rights of Indigenous Peoples was adopted in 2007, Article 22 included protections for women and children in regions of armed conflict. The violence became understood in its context of historic discrimination where the people were often displaced from homelands and had limited access to justice relevant to their culture.

In summer 2010 nearly 2,000 indigenous representatives from around the world gathered at the UN headquarters in New York City for the ninth session of the Permanent Forum on Indigenous Issues. From the United Sates, forum member Tonya Gonnella Frichner from the Onondaga Nation presented a preliminary study, "Doctrine of Discovery: Legal Construct Historical Root," that had just been completed.

"This is why indigenous peoples had been experiencing, describing, and fighting for more than five centuries," Tonya said. "We already see signs of ecological collapse in the over consumption of fisheries, massive deforestation, toxic chemicals spewed across the earth and into waterways."[5]

Murray Sinclair, Chairperson of the Truth and Reconciliation Commission of Canada, said that Canada's indigenous peoples had experienced harm for more than 150 years with the enforcement of assimilation through the use of Indian residential schools in the nineteenth and twentieth centuries.

---

4. International Labour Conference, "Spotlight on Domestic Workers Convention."

5. Economic and Social Council, "Preliminary Study."

The Longhouse

"The Canadian government stated early on that, through their policy of assimilation, within a century Indian people would cease to exist," he said.

Member of the Forum, Margaret Lokawua, from Uganda, said the Doctrine affected people in Africa. She said that western philosophy essentially said, "You go stand over there, close your eyes and pray while we take your land." Traditional courts were no longer recognized. Traditional education had been destroyed.

Hassan Id Balkassm, Forum member from Morocco, spoke of children placed in schools seeing their cultures destroyed. He said in North African schools had not taken into consideration indigenous peoples' identities and had imposed assimilation policies. Children were made to feel guilty for speaking in their own language.

Kaab Malik of the Indigenous Peoples Survival Foundation shared thoughts about indigenous people facing the same struggle to protect Mother Earth, their languages, and their ways of life. He was concerned about the devastating impact of development pushing climate change on indigenous communities in Pakistan, forcing them to change their traditional ways of life.

Carlos Samara, Vice-Minister of Indigenous Issues of Venezuela, said, "We are rebuilding what had been destroyed by the capitalist world." Urging cooperative protection of biodiversity especially in the Amazon, he said, "All leaders should hear the voice of our peoples. Enough of things being imposed."

Kuriakose Bharanikulangara, observer for the Holy See, responded and told them the papal bulls have been abrogated over the centuries, the Church has upheld rights of indigenous peoples to their ancestral lands and the Vatican had refuted the discovery doctrine.

On May 29, 1537 Pope Paul III sent out a papal bull[6]: "To all faithful Christians to whom this writing may come, health in Christ our Lord and the apostolic benediction." His doctrine began with reminding that "God so loved the human race that he created man in such wise that he might participate, not only in the

6. Pope Paul III, "Sublimus Dei."

good that other creatures enjoy, but endowed him with capacity to attain to the inaccessible and invisible Supreme Good . . . Hence Christ, who is the Truth itself, that has never failed and can never fail, said to the preachers of the faith whom he chose for that office 'Go ye and teach all nations.' He said all, without exception, for all are capable of receiving the doctrines of the faith."

In this message, Pope Paul III instructed Christians that "whatever may have been or may be said to the contrary, the said Indians and all other people who may later be discovered by Christians, are by no means to be deprived of their liberty or the possession of their property, even though they be outside the faith of Jesus Christ; and that they may and should, freely and legitimately, enjoy their liberty and the possession of their property; nor should they be in any way enslaved."

He saw the enemy of God at work in treatment of native people had "invented a means never before heard of, by which he might hinder the preaching of God's word of Salvation to the people: he inspired his satellites who, to please him, have not hesitated to publish abroad that the Indians of the West and the South, and other people of whom We have recent knowledge should be treated as dumb brutes created for our service."

In the creation of humanity people were given distinct heritage, an identity that God fostered to be in relationship with him. Follow no man, Paul told believers. No other has died for us to break bondage, defeat the loss that death causes, no other name can forever banish the dark, no other has the power to redeem us. With unsurpassable joy Jesus said to his disciples:

"I am the way and the truth and the life. No one comes to the Father except through me."

"I am the gate; whoever enters through me will be saved."

"I am the resurrection and the life. The one who believes in me will live."

The fields are ripe for the harvest.

Recognizing we are each part with God's creation, the Anishinaawbe grandmothers, a group of native women in northern US and South Central Canada began an annual walk for the water in

The Longhouse

2003. Beginning at a spring they walked around Lake Superior to bring awareness of the water's suffering in wetlands, rivers, lakes, and salt oceans. They walked Lake Michigan the next year then Lake Huron, Lake Ontario, Lake Erie, and followed the flow as the Great Lakes emptied into the St. Lawrence River. They walked the St. Lawrence and came through Akwesasne. As the season renewed again in 2013 they walked part of the Mississippi River.

Their walk brought groups together with them making campsites, preparing food, and sharing their stories. By respecting the design and gift of each body of water, they reminded people it will care for us. Technology integrated with the guidance of ceremonies, mindful of the opportunity we have been given to work together, they tell us water is alive, a member of creation, listening to us, responding to us, and requiring our respect.

In the north, St. Lawrence Island, surrounded by the Bering Sea west of mainland Alaska, sits just 150 miles south of the Arctic Circle and miles away from any industry or agriculture. The Yup'ik people thrived here for generations, sustained by greens, berries, fish, and marine mammals. In the 1980s the 1,600 residents began noticing family and friends were not well. They began to see cancer, low birth weights, heart disease, and miscarriages afflict their people. Pamela Miller, a research biologist, began working with the Yup'ik and established the Alaska Community Action on Toxics in 1997 to begin studies of environmental causes of the high rates of illness.

"We have ten times the cancer than the national average," said Vi Waghiyi, a Yup'ik resident of the island. A grandmother, she became ACAT's environmental health and justice program director to advocate for justice. She travels from her island home to speak at the UN's Permanent Forum and build coalitions. "Our women are concerned about learning disabilities. We have more learning disabilities than the lower 48 and higher mortality rates."

Dr. David Carpenter, director of the Institute for Health and Environment at the State University at Albany in New York, completed a study in 2011 revealing PCBs in the blood of the Yup'ik are about four times higher than the national average. The study found oils of the bowhead whale, seals, and walrus, a main food source, contained PCB concentrations of 193 to 421 parts per billion. The US EPA recommendation on consumption limits PCBs in fish to 1.5 parts per billion.[7]

"If a farmer in South America applies pesticide to his crops, within five to seven days it's up here in our backyard," Vi said.

Air pollutants come in on the wind currents from Asia and North America. Polychlorinated biphenyls (PCBs), organochlorine pesticides, and other chemicals carried in on the water are settling where the cold climate acts like a sink for the pollutants.

"This has become our reality," she said.

From her window Vi can see Russia, just thirty miles away.

"My dad was in the National Guard, our people helped rescue downed planes, we have young in the military," she said. "We have patriotism. For the military to do this is disheartening." The US Air Force established a base at the island's Northeast Cape in 1952. When they closed in the early 1970s, they left behind about 34 contaminated sites across a 9-mile-square area. Some 220,000 gallons of spilled fuel along with heavy metals, asbestos, solvents, and PCBs seeped into the land and water. One dumpsite held more than 29,500 buried drums. Bales of copper wire were abandoned, left to trap reindeer who died of starvation. The Army Corp of Engineers began remediating the site in the early 1990s.

Western science is finally accepting traditional knowledge about the environment, Vi said. "However when it comes to health, there's still a disparity."

The health care system for residents of St. Lawrence Island is 120 miles away in Nome. Vi said her people are given a lot of information about not smoking or drinking and not being sedentary. However, they are not a sedentary people; for example, they take skiffs out on the water to capture 60-foot whales weighing up to one hundred tons.

"Our traditional food is killing our people," Vi, said. "It's our identity. We're not going to stop eating our traditional foods. It sustains us, our spirit, physically and culturally." Because of global

---

7. Miller et al., "Community-based Participatory Research Projects."

The Longhouse

warming melting the ice, "Our men have to go further out into more dangerous storms to hunt," she said. The women once gladly nurtured the children when the food was brought in, but they now fear they could be causing their children harm just by feeding them.

"I never knew there was such injustice." Vi said. "Our children will lose knowledge if we lose our relationship to our foods."

Water covers more than 70 percent of earth's surface. Less than 3 percent of the water is fresh water, much of which is in snow or glaciers. All of humanity and the animals, plants, birds, and aquatic life depend on the 3 percent available. An estimated 46 percent of America's lakes and rivers are so poisoned they can no longer be fished, no longer provide swimming or sustain aquatic life, according to the UN's World Water Assessment Program.[8]

The pollution comes from 1.2 trillion gallons of untreated sewage, storm water, and industrial waste discharging into water every year. Half the world suffers from no clean drinking water contracting 250 million cases of water-based diseases. Millions of people die.

In 2010, a massive BP oil spill polluted land and water 125 miles off the Louisiana coast. More than a thousand birds, turtles, and mammals died. That same year the Transocean Oil Rig exploded in the Gulf of Mexico. Dead fish, birds, and dolphins wash up on the beaches. Their habitat that sustained them became poison. Chemicals like lead, cadmium, mercury, and PCBs are eaten by invertebrate that are consumed by fish, entering the food chain of people. People get hepatitis. Cholera breaks out in some nations. The interaction of living beings that depend on each other to continue life is destroyed. Entire ecosystems are being killed.

Preserving a healthy earth and people is requiring the knowledge of both western science and ancient knowledge to come together. The same shared knowledge is addressing the poisons destroying the bonds of respect toward women and children. Warning us these days would come, God spoke a promise through his prophet Isaiah.

8. World Water Assessment Programme, "Water in a Changing World."

For I will pour water on the thirsty land, and streams on the dry ground. I will pour out my Spirit on your offspring, and my blessing on your descendants (Isa 44:3).

You will be like a well-watered garden, like a spring whose waters never fail (Isa 58:11).

The women intuitively knew they were to be springs of water. In Canada, Sisters In Spirit became an initiative led by aboriginal women on behalf of the high rates of violence against the mothers, the daughters, sisters, aunts, and grandmothers in their communities. In 2005 they were networking across the country and learned that hundreds of women and young girls were missing or murdered. Investigating the cause, they spoke together as mothers and daughters, sisters and friends and saw the need to strengthen their tightly woven family systems that colonialism that had broken down.

In April 1990 the Native Women's Association of Canada had affirmed: "It is our Aboriginal women that represent the greatest disadvantaged group in all of Canada." They are seen as "other" and did not always elicit empathy by middle classes who sometimes blamed them because they lived a different lifestyle than their own.

As the distress entered non-native communities the women took hold of each other's hands with vigils and gatherings held across the US and Canada for the missing or murdered women. The gatherings raise awareness and push for investigations. Many stories came out about childhood violence. Some like Millie's were from birth families. Many happened in foster homes and juvenile institutions.

By November 2008, they confirmed 511 cases—25 percent missing and 67 percent murdered women. No one had been arrested or charged in 58 percent of the cases, compared to the 15 percent of similar cases against non-native women.

Their voice was joined by other organizations—Amnesty International, the Anglican Church of Canada, United Church of Canada, Women's Inter-Church Council of Canada, Battered Women's Support Services, and the Royal Canadian Mounted

The Longhouse

Police to name a few. A youth representative in every provincial and territory association fosters young women to know about the dangers as well as reinforcing the safety found in their own heritage. More than half of the missing and murdered women had been under thirty years old. At least 22.7 percent had one or more children.

What happened to those children?

A daughter glimpses herself reflected in the expressions of her mother's face. Attachment forms to loving and intuitive mothers, promoting a sense of being worthy of affection and being listened to. If it's absent, unreliable or as in Millie's case, if what's reflected is cruel, then a void of uncertainty is left. Relationship is unreliable. Emotional connection is an unprotected place to be. No amount of validation from husband or friends changed this for Millie. The void aches for attachment and in its search there is an attempt to stifle self and try to please someone else. Boundaries are not perceived. The message of who a woman is to God is stifled beneath layers of dust. The constant search led Millie to repeat relationship dynamics but true intimacy was never found. She is dismissed as being distant or defensive.

Millie remembers every scathing word her mother said to her. She carries every helpless rage her brother caused her. To outsiders, it seems easy to say just throw it off and hold yourself together.

"If I cry out concerning wrong, I am not heard. If I cry aloud, there is no justice" (Job 19:7).

Carrying her mother's view of herself, she felt that it is she who is not enough. There's distrust of her value.

"I am afraid of all my sufferings; I know that you will not hold me innocent" (Job 9: 28).

The day Millie looked at the cause of her wounds began her journey. She came to the circle of women and began to have her sight clear, her hearing discern, and her words heard. This is the balm, to soothe the wounded, preventing it deepening. There is no sense of pardon that another person can grant. Fear of judgment cannot be taken away. The wound is to the very soul.

Anger at being unprotected, a generation rose to pace about restlessly, disrespecting their elders, making decisions without the wisdoms of the grandparents. Relationships with mothers and fathers were disrupted. Earth degraded rapidly in that generation, following a new structure of lifestyles that pushed the agenda of "me."

Grandparents watched this storm of rebellion break apart their lineage and take away youth that would have been with them in their old age. Like Anna, many of the older women were past the cares of building a home, raising children, or deciding a work to do. Their hearts now are fully focused on relationship with Creator.

"The widow who is really in need and left all alone puts her hope in God and continues night and day to pray and to ask God for help" (1 Tim 5:5).

The Council of Thirteen Grandmothers formed in 2004 as a fountain of prayer, education, and streams of healing for all earth's inhabitants by supporting the lessons of their ancestors to guide through the uncertain future. Twice each year the grandmothers meet in each other's homelands of Nepal, the USA, Canada, Africa, Brazil, Nicaragua, and Mexico with hundreds of participants joining them from around the world. They learn of each other's cultures and new ways to bring change to their communities. They are responding to centuries of persecution when their spiritual knowledge carried on in secret to survive penalties of death.

Christians are coming into this same oppressive experience. In more than sixty countries Christians are being persecuted for their faith. In some of these nations it is illegal to own a Bible, to share faith in Christ or teach your children about Jesus. Women of faith are being told by their own religion to blur the line between boys and girls. Compromise of God's message is everywhere. One of the last instructions Jesus gave his disciples was to love one another because we will desperately need each other. The day is closing in when to be unyielding to the mainstream, in the same way traditional elders have continued knowledge, will mean to become a community in shared struggle. The last warnings Jesus gave his disciples were about the afflictions of hardship in the final days. Those who follow Christ despite opposition will be harassed, arrested, tortured, or killed. They may go hungry and be homeless. Yet his message continues, unstoppable.

> *I got to the point of being ashamed and then talking about what happened to me, and maybe too much. I think sometimes we can be too honest. But at the same time I feel like I have so much to hide.*

Our foe's weapon is discouragement—look what you've done, see your mistakes. God is not excusing the mistakes. God cannot overlook this. He is holy and we are separated from him. Holiness wants what is just before we can be reconciled. In his great understanding of our brokenness, he provided propitiation for our failings no matter how small or large a stumble. Christ took it on himself and justice was satisfied. We did not earn this. It was a gift.

"But if anybody does sin, we have one who speaks to the Father in our defense. We have an advocate with the Father, Jesus Christ the righteous one" (1 John 2:2).

There is one mediator.

"And my hope is in you all day long" (Ps 25:5).

Peacemaker didn't just cancel out bad behaviors. He planted better ideas to occupy lives so no matter how daunting the day, the people were aware of all they've been given.

"Create in me a pure heart, O God, and renew a steadfast spirit within me" (Ps 51:10).

Women from the Great Lakes, the St. Lawrence River, salt oceans, prairie creeks, swamps, and fresh springs all told of their experiences of water bringing a capacity for life. In the spirit of water, they say is the spirit of a new child within the water in the womb that is critical to care for during the months of gestation. Father and mother together nourish this care.

The water continues to fulfill its assignment, dropping from the sky onto earth, flowing into streams and lagoons leading out to sea or filling aquifers. The sun shines onto the lakes, the oceans, or finding it on leaves of plants and evaporates it, pulling it up into clouds. The wind comes bringing rain to us in a cycle begun at creation's first rainfall. When winter blankets the land and silences the flow of water, the peace tree remains, an evergreen covenant with the memories that draw home the wounded.

7

Mothers of Nations

Not one of his family or supporters ever thought that maybe he should stop his behavior but instead blamed it on the people he hurt or affected. His ex-wife was labeled as a scorned woman because she told the truth about what he did. And he stated that the girl lied about what he did to her. I'm sure he blamed what he did to the young girls on them simply for being around him. I know I should just get over it but I never dreamt it would be as bad as I found out.

—Millie

Two thousand years ago a Hebrew woman, Joanna, had a life of comfort. She was married to a rich man but she was unwell. The moment Jesus healed her she began to follow him into hardship. Recognizing he was the long-awaited promise of God, she used her wealth to provide travel, food, and protections for Jesus. In Luke 8:1–3 she is mentioned with Mary Magdalene and Susanna who devoted their lives to helping this new healer.

Journey to the Edge of the Woods

Many women were there, watching from a distance. They had followed Jesus from Galilee to care for his needs (Matt 27:55).

The women were among the first to see the risen Christ and bring the news to a suffering world. The heaviness in Eve's heart would be assuaged for all time through the line of humanity birthed through her to restore the balance of her mistake. Women worldwide would understand Ruth, the childless widow from another time in history who needed a kinsman-redeemer. Elizabeth, who waited so long for God to respond to the darkness of her ache, would welcome the new light. Tamar, whose beauty was stolen and trampled, or Miriam, who overcame the humanness of moods to watch over her brother and lead the women to rejoice, or Anna, who visited the temple desperate to see the fulfillment of prophecy, or Joanna, who took on the persecution and used her gift to open doorways for the good news to continue.

Jesus loved them all. To all, he responded with a justice that Millie could not find.

The constitution of the Great Law that Millie lived under is embedded with a legal system. Historically, this meant those who wouldn't change how they brought harm were banished in order to protect the community. Relatives brought sanctions of shame because offenses are not against a state or federal law. Offenses are against kinship. Justice is about relationship.

Justice became defined more as laws in the 1930s as states began taking more control over legal matters on reservations. Banishment today means an offender is in the hands of the non-native police department in nearby towns. Women's roles became about equal pay based on a culture fostered by an attitude of consumerism. Women were reduced to being seen as commodities a man is entitled to own. David Lisak, a former professor of psychology at the University of Massachusetts in Boston, conducted a 2002 study of 1,882 male students at a mid-size college, gathering data on the rising incidents of sexual assault on campuses. His study, *Repeat Rape and Multiple Offending Among Undetected Rapists*,[1] disclosed 120 of the men, about 6 percent, were responsible for

---

1. Lisak and Miller, "Repeat Rape."

1,225 rapes. Spiking drinks with alcohol or drugs was a frequent finding, as was choosing victims among their own peers who could be considered acquiescing if court were to prosecute.

The study noted their proclivity for being around other men who had the same attitude toward women. They wanted the approval of other men. Boys who grow up without a bond to good men modeling good minds find encouragement in the spreading darkness of exploitation.

By 2006, the UN Working Group on Trafficking on Human Beings estimated 4 million victims every year, 80 percent of them children and women, most sold to other countries for sexual exploitation. Pushed by global economics and widening gaps between rich and poor countries, these women and children are held as slaves in prostitution rings for military encampments, child pornography, slave labor, sweat shops, illegal adoptions, forced pregnancies, unwanted marriages, or for the sale of internal organs on the black market.

In wealthier countries searching for independent self-fulfillment marginalized women's importance as daughters, sisters, wives, and mothers. Being nurturers of life, influential to the character of the next generation became less valued than employment and income. Shrouded in wounds from divorce, single parenting, resentments and guilt, the message of the life of Christ as one of sacred covenant to serve others was overshadowed with a quest for personal rights.

Problems worsened despite the government repeatedly forming task forces. In 2001 there were ten females from Akwesasne in the county jail. In 2010 there were thirty-two. Sixty percent of those participating in Akwesasne's Healing to Wellness drug court are mothers with children. All are said to have sustained childhood trauma.

Steps taken from prevention to healing began restoring justice in terms of relationship through the many aspects that need to work together. Healing to Wellness shares joint jurisdiction between the St. Regis Mohawk Tribe and the state with an agreement between the tribe's court, town of Bombay and the

Franklin County DA's office. The Mohawk Council of Akwesasne also forged a cooperative agreement with the Canadian jurisdictions, bringing their police, health, and justice services to work together. On the south shores, SRMT's Chief Judge PJ Herne, Hawi from the Konon:kwe Council, representatives from the health services, probation department, public defender's office, and alcohol dependency programs work together, phasing an offender out of the system and into a stable life. It provides for the first time a system from within the community that acts in collaboration with the surrounding culture for the well being of both families.

The Indian Law Resource Center reports some 88 percent of crimes against native women are committed by non-natives who knew there would be little consequence. Leaders of native communities had no legal way to protect the women or prosecute offenders.

"This leaves Indian nations, which have sovereignty over their territories and people, as the only governments in America without jurisdiction and the local control needed to combat such violence in their communities," Terri Henry reported, member of the Indian Law Resource Center and Councilwoman of the Eastern Band of Cherokee Indians.

Tribal leaders came into partnership with the advocacy groups from battered women's movements, law enforcement, victim services, and prosecutor's offices who began the Violence Against Women Act in the late 1980s. On March 7, 2013, VAWA was signed to authorize tribes to investigate, prosecute, convict, and sentence non-Indians committing acts of domestic or dating violence, or violating orders of protection in Indian country.

The Indian Law Resource Center, the National Congress of American Indians Task Force on Violence Against Women, Clan Star, Inc., National Indigenous Women's Resource Center, and other native women's organizations had turned to the international human rights community for support.

In 2011, Rashida Manjoo, UN Special Rapporteur on the Rights of Women, presented her report to the UN General Assembly in New York telling the United States to "consider restoring

... tribal authority to enforce tribal law over all perpetrators, both native and non-native, who commit acts of sexual and domestic violence within their jurisdiction."[2]

James Anaya, UN Special Rapporteur on the Rights of Indigenous Peoples, toured Indian territories for a month in 2012 and at the UN Human Rights Council in Geneva recommended the US make it an immediate priority to legislate protecting native women. Again in February 2013, Rashico Manjoo and James Anaya urged the House of Representatives to approve the revised bill.

> *It all depends on community members wanting justice or showing concern and wanting to prevent others from being hurt. It takes someone to have to push and no one is doing that in his county. I may have overreacted but at least I reacted when others chose to ignore his behaviors. I still don't believe his behavior can be trusted and there is still the potential for sexual abuse of minors because he preys on young girls in bars as told to me by a community member there.*

Reluctance to believe justice will be found by going to court is not without merit. Cases compiled by Transactional Records and Clearinghouse at Syracuse University found that in 2011 federal prosecutors declined to file charges in 61 percent of cases involving sexual abuse of children on Indian reservations, compared to 20 percent of drug trafficking cases. But it's not where the major breakdown occurs.

> *When we're talking about the welfare of children we're really talking about the well being of the adults around them.*

There have been years of programs taken up by communities teaching us to recognize warning signs and protect the vulnerability of children, including cross-cultural partnerships with Child Advocacy Centers, rehabs for drug and alcohol abuse, women's shelters, foster care, and traditional healing programs. Many communities have an impressive number of programs in place to

---

2. Manjoo, "Statement."

strengthen youth. And still the problem of untold victims remains a hidden terrible pain.

> *It's hard to understand why so many knew but didn't come forward. What I didn't understand is why none of it was reported to police. People are saying he raped an eight-year-old and no one went to the police even though she told. The victims never got any kind of support and I doubt they ever will.*

In talking with others about the abuse that had continued so long, Millie received this email from another one of B's victims:

> B is responsible for all of our pain. It has been very difficult for me these last few days but that's not your fault. I'm glad you've been speaking out. Believe me I know how hard that is. I'm very glad something was done (i.e., his job) but I hope there will be more to come. I wish you luck with your personal journey. It has taken me a very long time and a lot to counseling and clearly I still have difficultly. If I can offer a bit of advice try to work on your pain sooner than later. I spent a lot of time hating and being so angry that I missed out on some of my life. That gives him more power over us and he's not worth it. I know like me you know all this in your head but making our feeling follow is the hard part. I will talk to you soon stay strong.

> *I really don't see any banishment of any kind going on. I think the most we can expect that might happen might be that the funding for their projects stops. It isn't council run so if they stopped funding it would make it hard for him to continue unless the directors take it upon themselves to speak up and to say they do not want him to be around the children due to his past charge a sex offender.*

One of the program coordinators responded to Millie:

> Thanks again, I am planning to meet with someone this week to discuss. Yes it has shocked me to a point as we had to let B go after learning he had charges of sexual abuse and our policy is workers cannot be around children or elders with those charges whether the outcome is

a level 1-2-or 3 predator. If anyone is willing to talk with me it would be helpful. Like I said, as long as hard facts can be proven then we can certainly raise the issue to our communities and definitely keep them away from Nation buildings and grounds.

There is no one who will hold him accountable. There is no justice she could find.

> *I don't see him as the kind of individual who would take responsibility for his actions, only make excuses for them. He's had too many people supporting his actions and projecting all blame onto others that he will go to his grave and beyond feeling and thinking that his behavior was acceptable as he stated, "Because I could." Narcissism at its most profound. It seems to be a character flaw I have to find men who are distant then I work to try and make them like me. Sounds pathetic, I know.*

When Peacemaker saw Aiionwatha sunk deep in his grief, he understood that to reach him, he needed to listen to what was meaningful to Aiionwatha. When circles are designed for a community to promote knowledge that fits their identity, it's much more likely to be sought and for men to know themselves as vital for children to grow secure and trust their leadership. Condolence is about every heartache, wiping every tear, giving clear water to drink with sensitivity to where a person is in their grief, and its effect in their community. Partnerships exist when each community defines its own priorities of issues. This can differ from one native community to another as each administers resources in their own roles as men and women.

Aiionwatha's forgiveness came when he fell into the arms of mercy to be given the purpose of reconciling others. This is our hope—a merciful God who moves across the fields with warm sunshine, awakening assurances that establish us in a new identity as part of a larger purpose beyond self.

With the sound of ice breaking, the thunderous rush of water breaking free, rushing over the rocks, purifying and replenishing along its way, we feel it melting our hardened minds to return to the cycle of life's currents again. Creeks and streams join our river coming from far and near and we are strengthened in our part of the life-flow pushing forward over roots firm in what was given and the elements of support surrounding us.

Life is reconciled again, budding from the earth. It has always been waiting, since time began, to bring us into purpose. Creator has been unchanging in his messages. Jesus said he would accept those who did what was right in every nation on earth. He had said the Word should be shared with every nation. Yet "the circumcised believers who had come with Peter were astonished that the gift of the Holy Spirit had been poured out even on Gentiles" (Acts 10:45).

The Great Mystery, the power that is God, fulfills his intent. The grandmothers see this. Their prayers are not for more possessions or a new goal for their own lives. Their gaze falls on their children's children and their great-grandchildren. Becoming ready to leave their lives, they more closely align with God perceiving a way to continue his instructions into each generation. They look out upon the future and their prayers fill with compassion for the lives that will be lived. For them justice means restoring relationship. It has nothing to do with a hierarchy of powers that will enforce or punish.

The last recorded words of Peter before he went to his death were, "But grow in the grace and knowledge of our Lord and Savior Jesus Christ. To him be glory both now and forever" (2 Pet 3:18). He came to understood the grace that had matured his impulsive decisions into a rock of tempered faith. He could forgive because he realized his own need of forgiveness. For those who believe God, mistakes and pain hold the knowledge of his grace.

Millie looked a last time at the ashes and regrets left from burning B's picture. The rituals, the ceremonies she attends, visiting the river of her ancestors, are all ways of holding onto what she knows can be trusted. Remembering the source of all good things is the source of each of us, the grandmothers were counseled by the created world to renew the compassions and the practice of giving thanks often because there will be relapses, knowing that our surge of moods are only that, moods that come and go in the physical world.

> *I'm doing really well these days. I had a new job offer which I turned down but they want to hire me as a consultant, I finished my program at a university with great academic standing and I've been feeling a lot better these days. I'm back with my husband and family and I know how much I have been given. I am thankful for what I do have in them. Of course it's not perfect but life never is.*

Just days later she says:

> *This thing that happened with B is bothering me way more than I realized. It's true when I was told I'm consumed. I'm in this somewhat dead relationship with my husband that I'm too scared to leave and I manage to mess up other relationships with my persistent badgering. And that's exactly what I do. Badger people to the point where I turn them off completely. I pushed someone to the point of him telling me to stop because stupid me continued to talk about those sex offenders. What the heck is wrong with me?! I admitted some things to him about me and B and how I was ashamed and even more so to discover his offense. Now this other co-worker just thinks I'm crazy and I don't blame him. Now I'm sure he's too disgusted with my behavior that he'll look at B as a victim. I don't know if he could've done anything anyway but I'm sure he won't now! It was plain stupid of me.*

The mind reaches to put the pieces back together but the body remains fearful because of the destruction. The spirit holds together the hope of mind and body. What Millie wanted was relationship of truth and recognition of herself as a woman. Even the life of Job in his devastation was healed by the return of family and friends around him.

Girls suffering sexual abuse rarely find gender responsive support although their social problems most often are from being in need rather than being a danger to others. Signaling a failing country, between 1991 and 2003 girls' juvenile detentions rose by 98 percent, compared to a 29 percent increase in boys' detentions,

Journey to the Edge of the Woods

according to the Georgetown Center on Poverty, Inequality and Public Policy.[3] They enter the system as victims of trauma, abuse, and neglect or from misdirection. The world is telling children there is no difference between male and female and they are left without direction to grow.

A child may not have the understanding to find words to speak about what's happening. Shame floods them, internalized into adulthood. Violence and wrong images of men and women surround their minds. Abuse leaves them paralyzed in grief ranging from depression and drug use to severe withdrawal. The message embedded is of lost worth.

Eighty percent of child deaths happen to children under three years old, nearly always at the hands of those responsible for their well being. Murder is the second leading cause of death for children the first ten years of their lives and young adults before twenty-four years of age. These 2012 studies from the Attorney General's Task Force on Children Exposed to Violence found homicide of young children under the age of four rose to 9 percent of deaths in 2008 from 7 percent in 1970. Suicide is the fifth leading cause of pre-adolescent children dying in the US. A culturally diverse group of people prepared the report, coming out of shared concern for our children and bringing knowledge and resources to each other. They came out of the federal and state governments, communities, and tribes across the country because the safe world for children is vanishing.[4]

Interacting with their environment is how the young learn to live. Being harmed or neglected imprints the neuro-pathways affecting ability to respond to relationship. The child without the nurturing of trust-producing serotonin, a chemical creating feelings of well being, lives with the sense of the world around them as unpredictable. Long term, this develops a life lived defensively. Survivors struggle with finding meaning in long talks about the Bible when it is far from realistic ways to protect themselves and feel safe again. As native pastors work with national and community

---

3. Watson and Edelman, "Juvenile Justice System for Girls."
4. Ibid.

healing, they stress the need for their people to hear the message of Jesus from the familiar voices of their own people in the context of their relevant issues.

By sitting down at their tables with daughters and granddaughters, the elders impart faith to see there is hope beyond the troubling times. The ways of the Great Mystery have been time-tested in their lives. Millie reaches into childhood and finds remembrance of trust in her grandmother. Her deepest tears welling up from childhood stopped the fruits of the anger and submissions against her own heart. The pain cries for lost security more than for courts of laws. Even as darkness lengthened into her days, she moved through shadowy woodlands teaching her the armor she needed to become like Solomon's soldiers, "all of them wearing the sword, all experienced in battle, each with his sword at his side, prepared for the terrors of the night" (Song 3:8).

"Before I was afflicted I went astray" brings about realizing the heart of God. Traditional justice is restorative, creating opportunities for amends to be made so both victim and offender reintegrate into the community. But damages from physical abuse are hidden and long-lasting. It cannot be undone. No payment eases the nightmare. The process of trust in relationship is shattered and with it, friendship and respect. When God restores, it is with comfort reflected in a grandmother's care, a mother's nurturing presence, the grandfathers whose voices bring a sense of all being well, a father's hand on a young shoulder making the world safe. He brings brothers and sisters to share the battleground and the celebrations because this is his best care in the design for humanity. We are healed through relationship.

In the center of a Haudenosaunee traditional village is the longhouse, representing the spiritual center of the community. Centuries ago it appeared to the newcomers to the land that men were in charge of all decision making. But the decisions spoken by the *roiane* carry the voice of the people. If a leader errs in upholding the governance of the Great Peace or attempts to make decisions without the approval of the people, it is the clan mother who warns him. So serious is it for a man to leave the way of life, she sends warnings three times to try to bring him back. The Great Law reminds that God's instructions cannot be changed. It was given to remain evergreen in the land even when all warmth and provision is buried in the cold. If he has not heeded her third warning, the women take the matter to the other *roiane* and the matter is named, the first step in a healing process. It is brought to the light that floods us with protections. A man is appointed to go with the clan mother and he removes the horns, the symbol of leadership, and says:

> "Behold the brightness of the Sun and in the brightness of the Sun's light I depose you of your title and remove the sacred emblem of your Lordship title. I remove from your brow the deer's antlers, which was the emblem of your position and token of your nobility. I now depose you and return the antlers to the women whose heritage they are."

Then he addresses the women, calling them Mothers and returns the emblem and title of the deposed leader to the clan mother.

Justice ultimately recognizes women's inherent right to raise healthy children in their own heritage. In 2014, Akwesasne students made a short video, "Young Haudenosaunee Men Respecting Women." The video showcased young men sitting together singing their ancient song that honors women. As they sang and beat the water drums, the young women danced the ancient women's dance. As they moved through the circle, they each took the hand of a girl who stood alone after she'd been mistreated and pulled her into the circle where her tired mind fixed on Creator helped her learn to dance again. As the men sang they pulled the abusive men into joining the song of honor.

Millie's children are fluent in their Mohawk language. She delights in her grandchildren. She breathes lightness seeing they are a part of her, safe and loved in their homes. She gives the encouragement that was not given to her as a child. She has put comfort in the landscape and it fills with a healing. The hardest burden remains in forgiving herself.

> *I've left my marriage yet again and I'm currently in a women's shelter trying to work on myself yet I'm in contact with a colleague which I know is not a good thing. I have a Facebook friend who has been wanting to hook up with me for several years but I'm afraid. He's a really great guy, very nice but I'm still too unsure of what to do. I've signed up for housing and I'll have to see where that goes. I need to know I can like me and be with me before I can be with anyone. Even my husband. But he also has to make some changes but is very unwilling to the extreme so I can only see myself continuing to be unhappy staying with him. What a life, huh?*

There may never be justice. But there can always be mercy. The court dismissed Millie's case that B had charged to silence her and no other charges were laid against him. She never saw justice enacted against the abuses. Still carrying the burden for having been in the wrong place or making the wrong choice, Millie struggles with the concept that mercy means we do not get what we deserve. Even to far reaching corners of the past when there is no way of returning across time to repair a wrong, God's glory will one day be seen forgiving someone in unmerited favor.

For there is one God and one Mediator between God and men, the Man Christ Jesus

(1 Tim 2:5).

When Millie burned the photo of B, she created a new memory. The flames shrunk his picture out of sight. The smoke lifted her prayer. She had made a choice for strength. There came a fragile comfort, a calm that would be disrupted by anger as she worked her way through it. In it is the battleground of her mind, the opposing balances taught in the story about the twin brothers of creation, filled always with both doubt and faith.

To a community struggling under loss of healthy foods, loss of safety for their children, loss of the strength of elders, the words "God loves you" will fall to the ground. There is already an everyday awareness of the presence of the Great Mystery that created life and provided a way for all life to live well. The meeting at the edge of the woods is Aiionwatha's first step toward healing. In it is the last instruction of Jesus when he spoke of the heavy persecutions coming to us. Feed the hungry, he said. Give a cup of cold water. Offer shelter and go to those who are hurting. It is the acknowledgment that we have tears we are too weak to carry by ourselves. We have wounds that are causing our souls to die. Healing doesn't change the past. Healing restores ability to be in relationship.

Cultures are coming from their weakness, needing each other because the waters are afflicted; women are absent from their value to communities, and the men wanting to protect children. People are coming alongside each other in agreement that God, the Creator, the Great Mystery, has designed instructions that are to be held like the *roiane* were instructed, planted with firm roots standing unmovable in the land even as the winds blow hard. This is the one blood we are brought into that runs like a river exalting songs of thanks in every language.

The respect, friendship, and peace that bind the Two Row treaty make it possible to share stories that build relationship. There will be no comfort for women like Millie until trust is rewoven. We bargain through the process of trauma until casting blame no longer eases the mind and we accept the reality. This happened. The reality is unbearable. No matter who is to blame, we begin to see our own responsibility is all any of us can carry. For non-natives walking on the territory of indigenous people, seen as uprooted, far from their land of origins, no longer knowing their original language or able to share knowledge of traditions or understand the importance of this ancestry, there are words that are forming relationship: "We need to protect a way for our children to be safe. Our women are hurting. We need each other to do this." Acknowledging our own weaknesses begins a sense of cleansing together.

Every morning a new life meets the sun, yet no matter how many births through the generations, there will be no other cry like the sound of God's son in the hills of Judah the night heaven opened to shine a light when Jesus came as an infant.

The last words Jesus spoke on the cross were, "It is finished." In the original language it was one word, translated to mean "it is paid in full," a word used to cancel a debt. Our debt. The disciples who changed the world speak of this: "Therefore, if anyone is in Christ, the new creation has come: The old has gone, the new is here!" (2 Cor 5:17). Even as we continue to walk through our earthly lives with memories, regrets, with unknown tears and unseen wounds, we learn to recognize the Shepherd's voice calling us to a new covenant.

And the gates of hell shall not prevail against us (Matt 16:18).

There is a broad path and the many walking in its many directions, humanism, political correctness, tolerance of every behavior, fear, or in belief every road is true. There is a narrow gate that requires us to put down our weapons and all the burdens we carry, and not all enter the gate. It does not mean the past is not with us. Revisiting the memories is how we understand the generosity of his sanctification and break wrong patterns that separated us from God and his body of believers. To those fallen in harrowing deep waters, those on this narrow path are the only ones who can bring that one light that heaven opened to us the night Christ was born.

More than a third of the world's women have reported experiencing violence, either sexual or physical. The UN Women's 2013 study reported that in some nations the abuse reports 70 percent of women. The study also reported 120 million girls worldwide, more than one in ten, have been raped or forced into sexual acts. In the United States, 83 percent of girls in grades eight through eleven, aged twelve to sixteen, have experienced sexual harassment in public schools.[5] Too many women and children are suffering. In their strength they are mothers of the nations, sisters, and daughters who hold the future of their people.

Therefore we will not fear, though the earth give way and the mountains fall into the heart of the sea (Ps 46:2).

For the Lamb at the center of the throne will be their shepherd; he will lead them to springs of living water. And God will wipe away every tear from their eyes (Rev 7:17).

He said to me: "To the thirsty I will give water without cost from the spring of the water of life" (Rev 21:6).

---

5. "Facts and Figures," *UN Women*.

Then the angel showed me the river of the water of life, as clear as crystal, flowing from the throne of God and of the Lamb (Rev 22:1).

Bibliography

Barreiro, Jose and Carol Cornelius. *Knowledge of the Elders: The Iroquois Condolence Cane Tradition*. Northeast Indian Quarterly. Ithaca, NY: Cornell University, 1991.
Basic Call to Consciousness, Rooseveltown, NY: Akwesasne Notes, 1986.
"Beyond the Shelter Doors: Advocate!" *National Indigenous Women's Resource Center*. Fall 2013. Web. http://www.niwrc.org/newsletters/11.2013/.
Bonvillain, Nancy. *Hiawatha: Founder of the Iroquois Confederacy*. New York: Chelsea House, 1992.
Broadrose, Brian. "The Haudenosaunee and the Trolls Under the Bridge: Digging Into the Culture of 'Iroquoianist' Studies." PhD diss., Binghamton University, 2014.
U.S. Supreme Court. "County of Oneida v. Oneida Indian Nation." *Find Case*. October 1, 1984. Web. http://caselaw.lp.findlaw.com/scripts/getcase.pl?court=US&vol=470&invol=226.
Cuffe, Sandra. "A Declaration of War: The Arming of Canadian Border Agents in Mohawk Territory." *Akwesasne Counterspin*. June 18, 2009. Web. https://akwesasnecounterspin.wordpress.com/tag/cbsa/.
DeMoss, Nancy Leigh. *Lies Women Believe and the Truth That Sets Them Free*. Chicago: Moody, 2006.
Department of Economic and Social Affairs Population Division. "Concise Report on the World Population Situation in 2014." *United Nations*. Web. http://www.un.org/en/development/desa/population/publications/pdf/trends/Concise%20Report%20on%20the%20World%20Population%20Situation%202014/en.pdf.
Economic and Social Council. "Preliminary Study Shows 'Doctrine of Discovery' Legal Construct Historical Root for Ongoing Violations of Indigenous Peoples' Rights, Permanent Forum Told." *United Nations*. April 27, 2010. Web. http://www.un.org/press/en/2010/hr5019.doc.htm.
Edwards, Jonathan. *The Life and Diary of David Brainerd*. Chicago: Moody, 1949.

Bibliography

"Facts and Figures: Ending Violence Against Women." *UN Women*. 2013. Web. http://www.unwomen.org/en/what-we-do/ending-violence-against-women/facts-and-figures.

Fadden, John Kahiones. *Haudenosaunee: Past, Present, Future. A Social Studies Resource Guide*. Albany, NY: University of the State of New York, 1988.

Franklin, Benjamin. "Excerpts from Speeches by Canassatego, an Iroquois, as printed by Benjamin Franklin, 1740s." *Smithsonian Source*. http://www.smithsoniansource.org/display/primarysource/viewdetails.aspx?PrimarySourceId=1195.

Gage, Matilda Joslyn. *Woman, Church, and State*. Reprint. New York: Arno, 1972.

George-Kanentiio, Douglas M. *Iroquois on Fire: A Voice From The Mohawk Nation*. Westport, CT: Praeger, 2006.

International Labour Conference. "A Spotlight on the Domestic Workers Convention and Recommendation." *UN NGLS*. June 16, 2011. Web. http://www.un-ngls.org/spip.php?page=article_s&id_article=3567http://www.unodc.org/documents/data-and-analysis/glotip/Trafficking_in_Persons_2012_web.pdfhttp://www.unodc.org/documents/data-and-analysis/glotip/Trafficking_in_Persons_2012_web.pdf.

Kaiser, Chris. "Sexual Violence Common Among Adolescents." *MedPage Today*. October 7, 2013. Web. http://www.medpagetoday.com/PublicHealthPolicy/PublicHealth/42129.

Kappler, Charles J., ed. "Treaty with the Mohawk, 1797." *Indian Affairs: Laws and Treaties*. March 29, 1797. Web. http://digital.library.okstate.edu/kappler/Vol2/treaties/moh0050.htm.

Keoke, Emory Dean and Kay Marie Porterfield. *Encyclopedia Of American Indian Contributions To The World*. New York: Facts On File, 2002.

Lisak, David, and Paul M. Miller. "Repeat Rape and Multiple Offending Among Undetected Rapists." *Violence and Victims* 17.1 (2002) 73–84.

Lyons, Oren and John Mohawk, eds. *Exiled in The Land of The Free: Democracy, Indian Nations, and The U.S. Constitution*. Santa Fe: Clear Light, 1992.

Manjoo, Rashida. "Statement by Ms. Rashida Manjoo, Special Rapporteur on Violence against Women, Its Causes and Consequences." *United Nations Commission on the Status of Women*. March 4, 2013. Web. http://www.un.org/womenwatch/daw/csw/csw57/statements/statement-rashida-manjoo.pdf.

McDonald, Thomas Michael. "The Black Book: Native Americans and the Christian Experience: Overcoming the Negative Impact of Nominal Christianity." PhD diss., Carolina University, 2004.

Miller, Pamela K. et al. "Community-based Participatory Research Projects and Policy Engagement to Protect Environmental Health on St. Lawrence Island, Alaska." *International Journal of Circumpolar Health* 72 (2013). Web. http://www.ncbi.nlm.nih.gov/pmc/articles/PMC3751231/.

Murphy, Gerald. "The Constitution of the Iroquois Nations." *Indigenous People*. Web. http://www.indigenouspeople.net/iroqcon.htm.

Bibliography

Pope Paul III. "Sublimus Dei." *Papal Encyclicals Online.* Web. http://www.papalencyclicals.net/Paul03/p3subli.htm.

Porter, Joy. *Land and Spirit in Native America.* Oxford: Praeger, 2012.

Porter, Tom, Lesley Forrester, and Ka-Hon-Hes. *And Grandma Said—Iroquois Teachings: As Passed Down through Oral Tradition.* Philadelphia: Xlibris, 2008.

Ptacek, James. *Restorative Justice and Violence Against Women.* Oxford: Oxford University Press, 2009.

Smith, Monique Gray. *Tilly: A Story of Hope and Resilience.* Winlaw, Britsh Columbia: Sono Nis, 2013.

Stanton, Elizabeth Cady. "The Antagonisms of the Sexes." *Current Opinion* 14.1 (1893) 259–61.

Swamp, Jake. *Giving Thanks: A Native American Good Morning Message.* New York: Lee & Low, 1995.

"Teenage American Girls' Suicide Rates Soar by 76 Percent." *News Medical.* September 9, 2007. Web. http://www.news-medical.net/news/2007/09/09/29571.aspx.

Tehanetorens (Ray Fadden). *Wampum Belts of the Iroquois.* Summertown, TN: Book Publishing, 1999.

UNICEF. "Breaking the Silence on Violence against Indigenous Girls, Adolescents and Young Women." *United Nations Population Fund.* May 2013. Web. http://www.unfpa.org/sites/default/files/resource-pdf/VAIWG_FINAL.pdf.

Venables, Robert W. *American Indian History: Five Centuries of Conflict & Coexistence.* 2 volumes. Santa Fe, NM: Clear Light, 2004.

Wagner, Sally Roesch. *Sisters In Spirit: Haudenosaunee (Iroquois) Influence on Early American Feminists.* Native Voices. Summertown, TN: Book Publishing, 2001.

Waldram, James, Ann D. Herring, and Kue T. Young. *Aboriginal Health in Canada: Historical, Cultural and Epidemiological Perspective.* Toronto: University of Toronto Press, 2006.

Watson, Liz, and Peter Edelman. "Improving the Juvenile Justice System for Girls: Lessons from the States." *Georgetown University Law Center.* October 2012. Web. http://www.law.georgetown.edu/academics/centers-institutes/poverty-inequality/upload/JDS_V1R4_Web_Singles.pdf.

World Water Assessment Programme. "The United Nations World Water Development Report 3: Water in a Changing World." *UNESCO.* Web. http://www.unesco.org/new/fileadmin/MULTIMEDIA/HQ/SC/pdf/WWDR3_Facts_and_Figures.pdf.

www.ingramcontent.com/pod-product-compliance
Lightning Source LLC
Chambersburg PA
CBHW072150160426
43197CB00012B/2326